The parables are some of the most  ...... Jesus, but many modern readers c. .... Why did Jesus teach like this? What was his message? Lee-Barnewall packs deep wisdom into this concise book, shedding light on context and unpacking how the parables are stories of divine grace.

Nijay K. Gupta
associate professor of New Testament,
Portland Seminary

Written with passion and candor, Michelle Lee-Barnewall investigates the parables' historical setting and invites readers to ponder their teachings in light of their own circumstances. She explains the puzzles in the parables as she develops their lessons on discipleship. This beautifully written exploration of the parables draws the reader to the feet of Jesus.

Lynn Cohick
provost and dean, professor of New Testament,
Denver Seminary

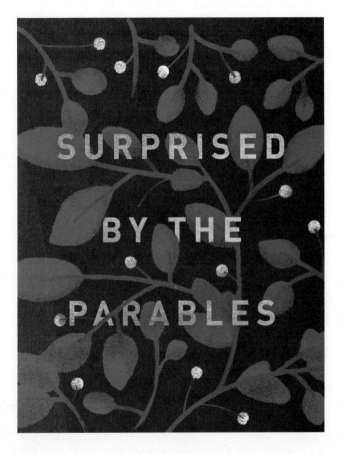

SURPRISED BY THE PARABLES

GROWING IN GRACE THROUGH
THE STORIES OF
JESUS

MICHELLE
LEE-BARNEWALL

SURPRISED
BY THE
PARABLES

GROWING IN GRACE THROUGH
THE STORIES OF JESUS

LEXHAM PRESS

Transformed by the Parables of Jesus: Growing in Grace through His Stories of Surprise

Copyright 2020 Michelle Lee-Barnewall
Lexham Press, 1313 Commercial St., Bellingham, WA 98225
LexhamPress.com

Unless otherwise noted, Scripture quotations are from the Holy Bible, NEW INTERNATIONAL VERSION®. Copyright © 1973, 1978, 1984, 2011 by Biblica, Inc. Used by permission. All rights reserved worldwide.

Print ISBN 9781683592990
Digital ISBN 9781683593003
Library of Congress Control Number:2019950882

Lexham Editorial: Derek R. Brown, Sarah Awa
Cover Design: Lydia Dahl
Typesetting: Sarah Vaughan

TO RHYS

A PRECIOUS GIFT OF
GOD'S GRACE.

CONTENTS

ACKNOWLEDGMENTS

This book represents a bit of a departure from my usual writing and research, and so I am very appreciative of the opportunity to pursue the project, first from Jim Weaver, and now from Lexham.

My friends and colleagues June Hetzel and Joanne Jung at Biola University provided support and encouragement especially in the early stages. My teaching assistant, Elaina Cray, read the entire manuscript and offered valuable critiques and suggestions.

For all writers and researchers, time is a most valuable commodity. A seventh-semester research leave from Biola gave me the time to complete the manuscript. Much-needed funding for the leave came from a Biola research and development grant and a grant from the Biola biblical and theological studies division.

My editor at Lexham, Derek Brown, kindly and enthusiastically guided me through the process and gave helpful feedback. I am grateful to him and everyone else at Lexham who has helped this project see the light of day.

And as always, I am very thankful for a patient and supportive husband who constantly encourages me to share my thoughts and write what I believe.

INTRODUCTION

One of my all-time favorite stories is O. Henry's "The Gift of the Magi." Set in the early 1900s, it tells the story of Della and Jim, a young couple who want to buy Christmas presents for each other, but have very little money. They do have two prized possessions: Jim's gold watch, which had belonged to his father and grandfather, and Della's long beautiful hair. Determined to give Jim something special, Della sells her hair in order to buy a platinum fob chain for the watch that he loves so much. She excitedly anticipates giving Jim his present, although with some concern about what he will think about what she has done with her hair.

The twist in the story is that Jim has just sold his watch in order to buy expensive jeweled combs for her hair, combs that she had so much wanted. Ironically, they each sold their most precious possession for the sake of the other person, who could no longer use the gift because they had also sacrificed their most prized belonging. Henry ends the story by explaining that the magi were wise men who brought gifts to the infant Jesus and that Della and Jim were similarly wise in their sacrificial gifts to each other. They chose selfless love as ultimately what was most valuable.

"The Gift of the Magi" is an example of a parable, which is often defined as a story used to illustrate a moral or spiritual lesson. The Gospels contain numerous parables, in which Jesus teaches about the kingdom of God and life in the kingdom. However, parables are also some of the most powerful means of spiritual formation, since they were intended not just to teach a lesson but also to confront and challenge the audience. Because of this, parables are uniquely suited to open our hearts to Jesus' transformative teaching and should be read—and experienced—in this way.

WHAT IS A PARABLE?

We generally think of parables as the stories that Jesus told. Our English word "parable" is the translation of both the Hebrew term *mashal* and the Greek term *parabolē*. In the New Testament, parables can also include similes (Matt 10:16, "I am sending you out like sheep among wolves. Therefore be as shrewd as snakes and as innocent as doves") and metaphors (John 10:7, "I am the gate for the sheep"). In the Old Testament, *mashal* can refer to proverbs (Prov 1:1), riddles (Ezek 17:2), and prophecies (Num 23:7).[1]

In this book we will focus on the parables that are stories. While all the parables give us glimpses into the kingdom of God, there is something that is particularly powerful about stories. In the story parables we see best how Jesus' teaching causes people to come to the point where they must decide whether their hearts will be open or closed to Jesus and the kingdom. The parables we will examine in this study focus on different aspects of Jesus' invitation to follow him in the hopes of challenging us to a more holistic understanding of what it means to be his disciple.

One critical item to remember in reading the parables is that they teach by transferring truth. This transference may be based on common knowledge. For example, when Jesus says, "The kingdom of heaven is like yeast that a woman took and mixed into about sixty pounds of flour until it worked all through the dough" (Matt 13:33),

---

1. "Parables," in *The Baker Illustrated Bible Dictionary*, ed. Tremper Longman III (Grand Rapids: Baker, 2013), 1266.

one can apply one's knowledge of bread making and properties of yeast to understand his point.

Story parables transfer truth through a focus on specific people and their actions.[2] So we evaluate the interaction of the judge with the widow in Luke 18:1–8. We consider the actions of the man who had two sons in the parable of the prodigal son (Luke 15:11–31). We follow the activity of the good Samaritan (Luke 10:25–37).

It is important to know that this transference is grounded in reality. This means historical context is critical to understanding the parables. Why does it matter that the hero in the parable of the good Samaritan is specifically a Samaritan? Why is it significant that the prodigal son asks not simply for money but for the inheritance? Is the friend who comes to the door in the middle of the night asking for food being rude or acting according to cultural convention? How should we expect the owner of the vineyard to act toward his workers? Sometimes parables make their point through exaggeration, but even then, the exaggerations emphasize the point based on the essential reality.

In parables, we try to identify what are called the points of reference. We look for areas that people would immediately identify with when they heard it. We need to know not just that two people passed by the man attacked by the robbers, but also that the two were a priest and a Levite. We understand the father in the story as a typical Jewish father and the sons as having normal filial obligations. By knowing the points of reference, we can identify the unexpected turn in the story. The points of reference set up expectations, and the unexpected turn creates a surprise, which is the deeper lesson of the parable, as Jesus confronts prejudices, brings about conviction, exposes hardness of heart, and so forth.

---

2. J. Dwight Pentecost, *The Parables of Jesus* (Grand Rapids: Zondervan, 1982), 8–10.

In many ways, parables are like jokes because they are not supposed to be interpreted as much as they are to be experienced. Jesus' audience would have known the points of reference, and so they would have gotten the point, or the twist, because they would instantly recognize what he was implying and when the story took an unexpected turn. They would have been in on the joke, so to speak. While we may not be able to relate to the story in the same immediate way as Jesus' audience, a greater knowledge of the points of reference moves us closer to hearing and experiencing the parables as they would have.

WHY DID JESUS TEACH IN PARABLES?

We can find the answer in Matthew's Gospel, where the disciples directly ask Jesus why he speaks in parables. Scripture tells us,

> The disciples came to him and asked, "Why do you speak to the people in parables?"
>
> He replied, "Because the knowledge of the secrets of the kingdom of heaven has been given to you, but not to them. Whoever has will be given more, and they will have an abundance. Whoever does not have, even what they have will be taken from them. This is why I speak to them in parables:
> "Though seeing, they do not see;
>> though hearing, they do not hear or
>> understand.
> In them is fulfilled the prophecy of Isaiah:
> "'You will be ever hearing but never
> understanding;
>> you will be ever seeing but never perceiving.
> For this people's heart has become calloused;

> they hardly hear with their ears,
> and they have closed their eyes.
> Otherwise they might see with their eyes,
> hear with their ears,
> understand with their hearts
> and turn, and I would heal them.'"
>
> (Matt 13:10–15)

Although the parables teach about the kingdom of heaven, the true message is only received by those who have willing hearts. Those who are open will seek Jesus for more clarification of the message, like the disciples do. Jesus calls them "blessed" because they are able to see and hear spiritual truths. However, those who are hardened will simply be confused or, even more, reject Jesus and his message. In this way, parables reveal God's secrets to some but conceal them from others. Indeed, for those who are unresponsive, even what they have will be taken away, and they will become even more hardened. The parables are teaching opportunities, but they also expose the nature of people's hearts. Jesus' use of Isaiah compares the crowds with Israel, who continually rejected God and his prophets. However, the disciples are blessed because they are able to grasp the nature of the kingdom of heaven.[3]

In this way the parables reveal to us a balance between a dependence on God's divine revelation and human effort. We must ultimately rely on God to reveal his truths to us. But it is also our responsibility to cultivate hearts that are open to his truths, even when they are painful and not what we might wish to hear at the moment.

---

3. Michael J. Wilkins, *Matthew*, NIV Application Commentary (Grand Rapids: Zondervan, 2004), 476–79.

The parables also serve as a warning. When presented with God's truth, we should not turn away! It is interesting to note that Jesus does not begin teaching with extended story parables until the incident with the Pharisees in Matthew 12, when they accuse Jesus of healing the demon-oppressed man by Beelzebul rather than the Holy Spirit. When they could not accept Jesus' more direct proclamations of truth, they found themselves even further from his life-giving message. We must be people who are willing to submit to God's truth, which means that the orientation of our hearts matters. Are we inclined to believe or be skeptical? Trust or turn away? Ultimately, are we open to God's work in us however he chooses?

WHAT TO EXPECT IN THIS STUDY

Parables not only teach a lesson; they also—perhaps even more impor-tantly—call for a response from the reader or hearer. Because of this call for a response, we need to keep in mind the original audience. We must always ask ourselves, Whom is Jesus telling the parable to? How did he challenge them? For example, we would expect a different reaction from a Pharisee, a Roman soldier, or a woman. Does Jesus intend to provide hope through the parable? Conviction? We need to know how he would have expected the audience to respond. This presents one of the challenges of interpreting parables because we need to be able to put ourselves in the place of the audience and imagine responding as they would.

However, this also provides a great opportunity for the transforma-tive impact of the parables. We may not be first-century Mediterranean people, but we can understand how the parables could affect them. Even more, we can get a powerful sense of the intended impact of the parable if we can translate it into our own context. Although we may not relate personally to the hostility a Jew would feel toward a Samaritan, we can consider an analogous situation in our own context to experience the same challenge that the audience would have felt in seeing a Samaritan as the hero of the story. We can look for the modern equivalent to the situation in the original parable.

The studies in this book are intended to help you discover the ancient world behind the story and then to guide you in applying it in your present situation. The chapters on the parables provide the background to the parables and explain how they would have been understood. The study questions will guide you into further reflection and can be used by individuals or in groups.

Each chapter highlights a different aspect of grace and the God who gives so generously. I hope that the Lord will use this book to meet you as you respond to the truth of God's grace in these stories. The parables contain rich teachings about the kingdom of God and what life in the kingdom is like. May the Lord bless you deeply as you dive into these teachings of Jesus.

THE JOY OF GRACE

*THE PARABLE OF THE LOST
SHEEP AND THE PARABLE OF
THE LOST COIN (LUKE 15:1–10)*

Now the tax collectors and sinners were all gathering around to hear Jesus. But the Pharisees and the teachers of the law muttered, "This man welcomes sinners and eats with them."

Then Jesus told them this parable: "Suppose one of you has a hundred sheep and loses one of them. Doesn't he leave the ninety-nine in the open country and go after the lost sheep until he finds it? And when he finds it, he joyfully puts it on his shoulders and goes home. Then he calls his friends and neighbors together and says, 'Rejoice with me; I have found my lost sheep.' I tell you that in the same way there will be more rejoicing in heaven over one sinner who repents than over ninety-nine righteous persons who do not need to repent.

"Or suppose a woman has ten silver coins and loses one. Doesn't she light a lamp, sweep the house and search carefully until she finds it? And when she finds

it, she calls her friends and neighbors together and says,
'Rejoice with me; I have found my lost coin.' In the same
way, I tell you, there is rejoicing in the presence of the
angels of God over one sinner who repents."

INTRODUCTION

A couple of months ago, my stepdaughter thought her dog had gotten out from her house. Frantic, she called my husband, who jumped into action, ready to rush over to help her look for the pup. Moments later, though, she called to say that all was well. She had forgotten that she had left him in a different bedroom while she was out. Overwhelmed at the thought that she might have lost her beloved pet, she broke down in tears.

A few days after that, my husband came home to find that the gate to the back yard was open. In a bit of a panic, realizing he had earlier let our golden retriever out of the house, he raced to the gate. To his relief he discovered the dog there, smiling happily at him (as golden retrievers tend to do) from just inside the open gate.

Both dogs were safe, but my stepdaughter's joy at finding what she thought had been lost was far greater than my husband's relief that the dog was not lost in the first place. Our joy at being reunited with something that had been separated from us also tells us how much that something means to us.

The parable of the lost sheep and the parable of the lost coin teach us about God's joy over finding the lost. In other words, they tell us what we mean to him. No matter what we have done, God's joy when we come back to him is overwhelming. In these parables, we see the Father's love and devotion. We also learn about the difficulty of the human heart in receiving such amazing grace.

THE PARABLES

In each parable, something valuable is lost, and a search is started. In the first parable, a shepherd has one hundred sheep and loses one. He leaves the ninety-nine in search of the missing animal. When he finds it, he rejoices and places it on his shoulders. He is so overjoyed that when he arrives home, he invites his friends and neighbors to celebrate with him. Jesus says that in a similar fashion, there is great joy in heaven over the sinner who repents, even more so than the ninety-nine who were not "lost" (Luke 15:6–7).

Jesus then tells another parable with a similar message. A woman who has ten silver coins and loses one will search her whole house diligently to find the missing coin. When she does find it, she will likewise call her friends and neighbors to rejoice with her, an action that is compared with the angels' rejoicing in heaven over the one sinner who repents.

Through the parables, we learn that God seeks after and rejoices after finding the lost. There is nothing on earth that can compare with God's joy over finding us when we have strayed from him.

THE AUDIENCE

In this passage Jesus is speaking to the Pharisees and teachers of the law, who are called scribes in some translations. These religious leaders complain because Jesus is spending time with tax collectors and "sinners." They think Jesus should reject these people, but Jesus teaches that he came to save those society rejects. He memorably illustrates this by telling two parables, using as main characters those who were looked down on by the larger society: that is, a shepherd and a woman. We will say more about shepherds and women later, but first let's take a closer look at the Pharisees.

The Pharisees appear quite often in the Gospels as Jesus' opponents. They were a Jewish religious party of laypeople thought to be experts in the law. Their concern was to define correct behavior according to the law.[1] Among all of the religious groups in Israel, they were probably the most popular and so were enormously influential among the general population.[2] The scribes were not as influential, and yet were similar to the Pharisees as professional interpreters and teachers of the law.[3]

Our general picture of the Pharisees and other Jewish religious leaders in the ancient Near East is often that they were hypocrites. Jesus calls them this six times in Matthew 23 alone! True, the Pharisees are rightly accused of breaking the very law they tell others to keep. However, this should not cause us to overlook the significance of their focus on the law. It is important to consider why the religious leaders placed so much emphasis on the law and why they might have been so legalistic.

To understand the Pharisees, we need to go back to the Old Testament, where God gave the law to Moses. The law became a critical foundation for God's relationship to Israel, and he tells them, "Now if you obey me fully and keep my covenant, then out of all nations you will be my treasured possession. Although the whole earth is mine, you will be for me a kingdom of priests and a holy nation" (Exod 19:5–6).

The law is God's gift to Israel because it represents how the nation is favored and chosen by God. It also shows them God's way of living, in contrast to the other nations, whom he has not chosen and so do not know the proper way to live. This is why the psalmist can say,

---

1. Steve Mason, "Pharisees," in *Eerdmans Dictionary of the Bible*, ed. David Noel Freedman (Grand Rapids: Eerdmans, 2000), 1043–45.

2. Michelle Lee-Barnewall, "Pharisees, Sadducees, and Essenes," in *The World of the New Testament*, ed. Joel B. Green and Lee Martin McDonald (Grand Rapids: Baker, 2013), 218–19.

3. Arland J. Hultgren, *The Parables of Jesus* (Grand Rapids: Eerdmans, 2000), 95; G. H. Twelftree, "Scribes," in *Dictionary of Jesus and the Gospels*, ed. Joel B. Green and Scot McKnight (Downers Grove, IL: InterVarsity, 1993), 732–35.

"Oh, how I love your law! I meditate on it all day long" (Ps 119:97), or "Great peace have those who love your law" (Ps 119:165). The law is a symbol of God's blessing on the nation.

However, we see that along with the privilege of being God's chosen people comes the obligation to obey the law. God tells Israel that he will bless them if they obey him and discipline them if they do not. "See, I am setting before you today a blessing and a curse— the blessing if you obey the commands of the LORD your God that I am giving you today; the curse if you disobey the commands of the LORD your God and turn from the way that I command you today by following other gods, which you have not known" (Deut 11:26–28).

Unfortunately, Israel does not obey the law, falling into immorality and idolatry, and so God curses them by allowing them to be conquered by other countries, Assyria and Babylon. After God brings them out of exile, they understandably try to follow the law with a renewed and impassioned desire to avoid being cursed by God again!

One key period after the exile exemplifies their rejuvenated attitude toward the law. During what was called the Maccabean Period (167–63 BC), the Jewish people faced an especially intense challenge to their way of life. During this time, Israel was under what was known as the Seleucid Empire. The ruler, Antiochus IV Epiphanes, put enormous pressure on the Jews to conform to Greek ways. He outlawed many practices that were important to the Jews, trying to get them to worship foreign gods and killing those who refused to eat unclean foods or who circumcised their children. Many Jews folded under such immense pressure, but others became even more determined to follow God's laws.

An ancient Jewish document called 1 Maccabees gives an account of how many Jews rebelled against their foreign rulers. It describes their persecution and determination to maintain the law, even at the cost of their lives:

> But many in Israel stood firm and were resolved in their hearts not to eat unclean food. They chose to die rather than to be defiled by food or to profane the holy covenant, and they did die. (1 Maccabees 1:63)[4]

> According to the decree, they put to death the women who had their children circumcised, and their families and those who circumcised them; and they hung the infants from their mothers' necks. (1 Maccabees 1:60–61)

During this time, many of the Jews suffered terribly in order to stay loyal to the law God had given them. What a contrast to the way Israel disobeyed God before the exile!

The cultural background makes it easier to understand why the law was so important to Israel, and it also helps us understand how the law could have been so easily abused. Israel became overvigilant in their determination to keep the law and avoid another situation like the exile. They came up with more rules that went beyond those given to Moses. Instead of practicing justice and mercy (Mic 6:8), religious leaders came up with a legalistic interpretation that weighed the people down with duties and obligations. They made the law a burden for the people rather than something to teach and guide them.

RESPONDING TO THE PARABLE

To forget about grace is a dangerous thing, because we all need it. We know we have received God's grace in the forgiveness of sins, but

---

4. First Maccabees is generally seen as having been written around 100 BC. See James C. VanderKam, *An Introduction to Early Judaism* (Eerdmans: Grand Rapids, 2001), 62.

grace should be something that changes our daily lives. But it is hard to receive God's grace and extend it to others, especially when we don't recognize how much we need it. This was the Pharisees' problem.

The Pharisees' zeal to do the "right" thing seemed to make it hard for them to empathize with those who struggled, and they ended up doing the "wrong" thing. It is probably no coincidence that Jesus gives two parables here about people who were considered either outcasts or inferior by the Pharisees.

The use of the shepherd puts the Pharisees in a particular bind. The Pharisees would want to identity with the hero of the stories, since they were supposed to be the leaders of the people. That this was Jesus' intent is also seen in the way he makes a direct connection with them, saying, "Suppose one of you ..." (Luke 15:4).

In general, shepherds were examples of those who were poor, uneducated, and lowly, close to the bottom of society's social ladder.[5] The average Jew considered them dishonest and lawless.[6] The Pharisees' obsession with obedience to the law would have caused them to see shepherds as unclean. So they would be offended to be referenced as one.[7] Certainly, no Pharisee would have been willing to work as a shepherd, and yet Jesus challenges them to imagine themselves as one!

---

5. Kenneth E. Bailey, *Jesus through Middle Eastern Eyes: Cultural Studies in the Gospels* (Downers Grove, IL: IVP Academic, 2008), 35; Darrell L. Bock, *Luke 1:1–9:50, Baker Exegetical Commentary on the New Testament* (Grand Rapids: Baker, 1994), 213–14.

6. Craig L. Blomberg, *Interpreting the Parables* (Downers Grove, IL: InterVarsity, 1990), 180.

7. Kenneth E. Bailey, *Poet & Peasant and Through Peasant Eyes*, combined ed. (Grand Rapids: Eerdmans, 1983), 147. There is some debate about the significance of shepherds, since the image of the shepherd can be used positively, as in Psalm 23, where the Lord is our Shepherd, or in the New Testament, where leaders are often called "shepherds" who lead the flock or congregation (e.g., 1 Pet 5:2). However, it is likely that here Luke is emphasizing the Pharisees' personal reaction to the current cultural assessment of shepherds, particularly since his Gospel emphasizes themes of the lowly and outcast.

The woman would also be a surprising hero of a parable. Jewish historian Josephus says bluntly that woman "is in all things inferior to the man" *(Against Apion* 2.201*)*. Women also had fewer rights. For example, according to Jewish law, only men could divorce, although in Rome and Greece both men and women could terminate the marriage.[8] Yet, Jesus chooses to make a woman the subject of this parable, using her to illustrate how diligently God searches for one who is lost and how much he rejoices when that person is found.

When Jesus compares the love of the Father to the actions of a shepherd and a woman, he challenges the Pharisees in their prejudicial and judgmental attitudes. If the Pharisees were willing to humble themselves to identify with these characters, they would learn much about the character of God.

While the Pharisees seemed to forget about grace, the need for grace would be a vivid memory for the "lost sheep." When Jesus refers to the ninety-nine "who do not need to repent," it's hard not to wonder, Is it really possible that someone does not need to repent? After all, Romans 3:23 says "all have sinned and fall short of the glory of God." Jesus seems to be taking aim at the Pharisees in another way here, since they apparently do not think they have any need to repent! Instead, it is the lost sheep who knows it is in need of rescue that Jesus places on his shoulders, brings home, and rejoices over. God's grace is available, but only to the heart that knows its need. Jesus not only confronts the Pharisees with their lack of grace, but also appears to indicate they

---

8. Everett Ferguson, *Backgrounds of Early Christianity,* 2nd ed. (Grand Rapids: Eerdmans, 1993), 69. Furthermore, there were various schools of thought as to acceptable conditions for divorce. The school of Shammai was more strict and only allowed divorce for sexual immorality, whereas the school of Hillel was much more lenient and permitted divorce for trivial matters such as burning one's husband's dinner. This appears to be the background behind the Pharisees' questioning of Jesus in Matt 19:3–12. See Michael J. Wilkins, *Matthew, NIV Application Commentary* (Grand Rapids: Zondervan, 2004), 642–43.

have not recognized their need for grace. Do we see and remember our own need for grace?

UNDERSTANDING GOD'S
PURSUIT OF US

Ultimately the parables are about understanding the heart of God. God does not pursue us because of our merit, but out of his grace and mercy. Tax collectors were despised because it was well known that they often abused the system by adding extensive surcharges to the Roman taxes they collected.[9] They were considered to be traitors for cooperating with the Romans and greedy because they collected more than was required.[10] In other words, they stood in stark contrast to Pharisees and their meticulous law keeping.

"Sinners" was a term that encompassed all of society's outcasts.[11] If you were one of these people, you would be painfully aware that you didn't measure up to the standards of the Pharisees, the ones who were supposed to know God's law. The tax collectors and "sinners" would probably have had no trouble seeing themselves as the lost sheep and lost coin. Imagine their surprise when Jesus tells everyone that the point is that you are the ones he is calling to be with him!

Unfortunately, in their zeal for the law, the Pharisees did not follow God's command to love their neighbor as themselves (Lev 19:18). Rather, they set themselves up as being superior and neglected those who were most in need of help. However, God, as the ultimate shepherd in the story, does the opposite. For a shepherd in that time, one hundred sheep would be a large flock, meaning that the shepherd would be fine if he lost one. But the shepherd cares deeply for that

---

9. Bock, *Luke 1:1–9:50*, 310–11.

10. "Tax Collector," in Longman, *Baker Illustrated Bible Dictionary*, 1605.

11. Pentecost, *Parables of Jesus*, 95.

single sheep and is willing to leave all the others to search for it.[12] He takes the burden of the lost sheep on himself as he lifts it onto his shoulders and carries it home (Luke 15:15).

God not only accepts sinners, but also pursues them. He longs to bring them back into his fold. When he finds the lost sheep, he does not scold or condemn it for wandering away, but invites all he knows to rejoice with him at its recovery. The finding of the lost sheep is a cause for celebration. No one had to tell my stepdaughter to rejoice when she found her "lost" dog. It came from her heart. God's grace is similarly a reflection of a heart that wants to be reunited with the object of his love—us.

LEARNING ABOUT GOD AND RECEIVING HIS GRACE

The amount of effort the main characters go to in order to achieve their goal of finding what is lost shows this love. The shepherd leaves the other ninety-nine sheep to seek the one who has wandered away.[13] Is the shepherd taking a great risk in leaving the ninety-nine in a dangerous situation, and potentially losing the flock, in order to save one? Or would it have been a normal practice to find a safe place for the rest of the flock, perhaps a sheepfold or cave, or leave them with someone else while he searched for the missing sheep? Whatever the reason, both situations reflect the importance of the sheep to the shepherd.

When the shepherd finds the sheep, he also demonstrates his care by putting the animal on his shoulders, probably wrapping the legs around his neck and then holding on to the legs. He might have done

---

12. Hultgren, *Parables of Jesus*, 53.

13. It is debatable whether Jesus really considered the possibility of a person who did not need to repent, even more whether the Pharisees would be considered righteous in this way. Most likely this is an ironic statement, since the entire Gospel indicates that Jesus considered all people lost.

this because the animal was terrified.[14] Being very social creatures, sheep are used to being with the flock. To be cut off is a very bewildering situation.[15] The story does not say whether the animal is also wounded, but it is clear that the shepherd is willing to take the extra burden of restoring the sheep.

The woman also goes to great lengths to find what is lost. She carefully searches her house for the lost coin, which would not have been an easy task. The floors, which would have been either dirt or stone, would have been covered with straw as protection against cold and dampness. This meant that the woman would have had to remove the straw and sift through it, then sweep the floor.[16] Finding the coin is a rather arduous affair, but it is valuable enough to make the effort worthwhile.

The efforts of both result in success, and such is everyone's joy that they cannot keep it to themselves but want to share it with others. The shepherd is so overjoyed at recovering the sheep that he is compelled to share his happiness with his friends and neighbors. Similarly, the woman calls those around her to rejoice with her. As we will see next in the parable of the prodigal son, the father does not simply welcome the son back, but throws a banquet in his honor, to which he invites the entire village. The overwhelming joy over finding what has been lost is a joy that wants to be shared.

This joy stands in stark contrast to the Pharisees' response. To both Jesus and the Pharisees, the "sinners" and tax collectors are indeed lost. Jesus wants to extend grace, but the religious leaders' response is to shun them. They might have done this in order to avoid the impression

---

14. David Wenham, *The Parables of Jesus* (Downers Grove, IL: InterVarsity, 1989), 100.

15. Simon J. Kistemaker, *The Parables: Understanding the Stories Jesus Told* (Grand Rapids: Baker, 1980), 172.

16. Pentecost, *Parables of Jesus*, 97.

of giving approval to their conduct.[17] The expectation would have been to draw firm boundaries between the righteous and the unrighteous to uphold the law, but Jesus breaks social convention by associating with and eating with them.[18]

Jesus sees people as created in the image of God, which means they are of great value. He sees their worth and responds to it. Jesus does not expect people to be sinless like he is. Instead, he is willing to meet them where they are. That is what grace is about. It lifts people from where they are, rather than crushing them for not attaining perfection. It provides dignity and hope. It gives life.

CONCLUSION: THE JOY OF GRACE

In his book *Mortal Lessons: Notes on the Art of Surgery*, Richard Selzer tells the story of a young woman who has just undergone surgery to remove a tumor in her face. As careful as he had been, Selzer had to cut one of the nerves in her face, leaving her mouth in permanent deformity, what he describes as "twisted in palsy, clownish." Selzer recounts the powerful conversation with the young woman and her husband as they face the reality of the pain and brokenness entering into their hopeful young lives:

> Her young husband is in the room. He stands on
> the opposite of the bed, and together they seem to
> dwell in the evening lamplight, isolated from me,

---

17. Hultgren, *Parables of Jesus*, 61. As Wilkins describes, "Table fellowship was an important social and religious convention among many groups in the ancient world. Boundaries were established that designated who were included and excluded from a meal, and that also served to delineate religious and ethical obligations toward the participants. Within Judaism … Pharisees were especially known for the role that table fellowship played in defining their group identities" (Wilkins, *Matthew*, 366).

18. Joel B. Green, *The Gospel of Luke*, New International Commentary on the New Testament (Grand Rapids: Eerdmans, 1997), 571.

private. Who are they, I ask myself, he and this wry-mouth I have made, who gaze and touch each other so generously, greedily? The young woman speaks.

"Will my mouth always be like this?" she asks.

"Yes," I say, "it will. It is because the nerve was cut."

She nods, and is silent. But the young man smiles.

"I like it," he says. "It is kind of cute."

All at once I *know* who he is. I understand, and I lower my gaze. One is not bold in an encounter with a god. Unmindful, he bends to kiss her crooked mouth, and I so close I can see how he twists his own lips to accommodate to hers, to show that their kiss still works. I remember that the gods appeared in ancient Greece as mortals, and I hold my breath and let the wonder in.[19]

I came across this story while reading Brennan Manning's *The Ragamuffin Gospel*. Manning compares the husband's contorting of his own mouth to meet his wife's with Christ's work of carrying our sin that we might be restored with God (2 Cor 5:21).[20] It is into the reality of our personal pain and brokenness that Jesus has entered, and Manning then asks: "What shall we say to such an outpouring of love? How shall we respond?"[21]

---

19. Richard Selzer, *Mortal Lessons: Notes on the Art of Surgery* (New York: Simon & Schuster, 1976), 45–46, italics original.

20. "God made him who had no sin to be sin for us, so that in him we might become the righteousness of God."

21. Brennan Manning, *The Ragamuffin Gospel* (Sisters, OR: Multnomah, 1990), 107–8.

In both parables, it does not really matter how the sheep and the coin were lost or how lost they were. What matters is that someone comes to find what is lost, and there is great joy at the finding. While we tend to focus on our sin, Jesus challenges us to focus on God and remember the grace he has given us. We can see God as someone who eternally calculates our flaws and how short we have fallen from what is demanded, or we can see God as the one who pursues us valiantly and is filled with joy when he finds us. When we see sin in ourselves and others, we can hide, deny, and condemn, or we can open our hearts so we can be found. God constantly offers grace, but what also matters is how we respond and receive it and the one who offers it to us.

MAJOR TAKEAWAYS

1. The parable of the lost sheep and the parable of the lost coin are wonderful lessons about God's grace. They take on a special meaning because Jesus tells them to the Pharisees, who did not understand the true nature of grace.

2. Because of Israel's past history of going into exile for their failure to keep the law, the Pharisees placed too much emphasis on doing the law instead of thinking about what the law really meant and what it taught them about God. They took something good and made it into something harmful.

3. In response, Jesus tells two parables, about a shepherd and a woman, reflecting his heart toward those who are often rejected by the larger society and how much God rejoices when the "lost" are found.

4. The Pharisees may have had a hard time accepting Jesus teaching because their emphasis on what they do leads them to be self-righteous. As a result, they are unable to see how much they too are lost and in need of being found.

5. The tax collectors and sinners accept God's transforming grace as they humbly recognize they are lost.

QUESTIONS

1. How hard does each of the main characters (the shepherd and the woman) work to find what they lost? What do you think motivates them to work so hard?

2. How does each one respond after they find the lost object? Why do you think they do this?

3. How would you describe the shepherd and what he does? Does this relate to how you understand God? Why or why not?

4. Jesus teaches us that God's grace is for people who are imperfect and don't fit societies' standards of who is successful and desirable. Are there ways you think you are undeserving of God's love and grace?

5. The Pharisees thought that their approach to the law was pleasing to God. The problem was they focused on following the law rather than softening their hearts to receive God's grace. They took something that was good and made it into something that harmed people. In what ways do you lean

toward self-righteous works to try to earn God's favor? What causes your heart to become hard? What can you learn from the Pharisees' example?

6. What do you think the parables teach us about God's desire for us and how important we are to him? How have you have seen God's pursuit of you in your own life?

7. Although the parable is about how God seeks the lost, it presents a larger picture of grace and the way God reaches out to us individually in love and acceptance. Do you ever find it difficult to accept his grace? Ask the Holy Spirit to help you accept the truth of God's lavish love and grace for you.

RECEIVING GRACE

*THE PARABLE OF THE PRODIGAL
SON (LUKE 15:11–32)*

Jesus continued: "There was a man who had two sons. The younger one said to his father, 'Father, give me my share of the estate.' So he divided his property between them.

"Not long after that, the younger son got together all he had, set off for a distant country and there squandered his wealth in wild living. After he had spent everything, there was a severe famine in that whole country, and he began to be in need. So he went and hired himself out to a citizen of that country, who sent him to his fields to feed pigs. He longed to fill his stomach with the pods that the pigs were eating, but no one gave him anything.

"When he came to his senses, he said, 'How many of my father's hired servants have food to spare, and here I am starving to death! I will set out and go back to my father and say to him: Father, I have sinned against heaven and against you. I am no longer worthy to be called your son; make me like one of your hired servants.' So he got up and went to his father.

"But while he was still a long way off, his father saw him and was filled with compassion for him; he ran to his son, threw his arms around him and kissed him.

"The son said to him, 'Father, I have sinned against heaven and against you. I am no longer worthy to be called your son.'

"But the father said to his servants, 'Quick! Bring the best robe and put it on him. Put a ring on his finger and sandals on his feet. Bring the fattened calf and kill it. Let's have a feast and celebrate. For this son of mine was dead and is alive again; he was lost and is found.' So they began to celebrate.

"Meanwhile, the older son was in the field. When he came near the house, he heard music and dancing. So he called one of the servants and asked him what was going on. 'Your brother has come,' he replied, 'and your father has killed the fattened calf because he has him back safe and sound.'

"The older brother became angry and refused to go in. So his father went out and pleaded with him. But he answered his father, 'Look! All these years I've been slaving for you and never disobeyed your orders. Yet you never gave me even a young goat so I could celebrate with my friends. But when this son of yours who has squandered your property with prostitutes comes home, you kill the fattened calf for him!'

"'My son,' the father said, 'you are always with me, and everything I have is yours. But we had to celebrate

*and be glad, because this brother of yours was dead and
is alive again; he was lost and is found.'"*

INTRODUCTION

Do you ever have the urge to splurge? You know your budget can't
afford it and you shouldn't do it, but you still go for the expensive
dress, the fancy dinner, or the new gadget. Or perhaps you are lavish
for someone else—you throw a big birthday bash for your best friend,
or take your spouse on that European trip they've dreamed of since
they were a child.

Prudence tells us that we should be careful how we spend our
money. It's good to save and not be wasteful. We feel guilty when we
spend more than we think we should. But at the same time, sometimes
it simply feels right to do something big. Your child wins first place
and you want to celebrate. Your spouse gets the promotion they've
been working toward for so long. These are the times when doing a
little more than is necessary shows how much we want to celebrate.
Celebration often requires extravagance, and we give freely and lavishly because we want the person to know how special they are to us.

We just read about God's determination to look for the lost sinner
and his joy when that person is found. God also lavishly celebrates in
the parable of the prodigal son. We'll take a look at this famous parable
to see what else we can learn about God's extravagant love.

THE PARABLE

The basic story is well known. A son approaches his father and asks for
his share of the inheritance. After getting what he wants, he promptly
leaves his father and squanders all of his money in a distant land.
Impoverished and starving, he finds himself feeding pigs and longing
to eat what they eat. He decides that he would be better off as a servant in his father's house than to continue in his desperate situation.

He resolves to return home to confess to his father that he has sinned against him, but as he approaches the house, the father runs to greet him. The father not only forgives him but orders a lavish celebration to be held in his honor since "this brother of yours was dead and is alive again; he was lost and is found" (Luke 15:24).

The parable is a marvelous story of the grace and loving acceptance of the father toward the younger son. There is also another part to the story when his older brother comes in from the field. When he hears the celebration and finds out that it is in honor of the returning younger son, he becomes enraged. He confronts his father. Although he has served faithfully all these years while the younger son wasted his money, it is the younger son who gets the celebration. How unfair! But the father reassures him that he does not lose anything because of what the other son has received, and all that the father has still belongs to him. Instead, he should focus on rejoicing with him in his brother's return.

THE FATHER'S GRACE AND THE YOUNGER SON

It is easy to see the younger son's offense. How could he be so greedy and so callously waste his father's money! The ancient context reveals an even deeper level of the son's offense.

The power of the parables comes not just from their use of everyday events and characters to teach a lesson, but sometimes from exaggerating normal customs.[1] There were times in which an inheritance might be distributed early in order to determine each person's portion so to avoid quarrels later on. However, it would never have been at the request of the heir, and especially not when the father was still in good health, which seems to be the case in this parable. To ask for

---

1. Klyne R. Snodgrass, *Stories with Intent: A Comprehensive Guide to the Parables of Jesus* (Grand Rapids: Eerdmans, 2008), 18.

the inheritance is essentially to wish for his father's death because the younger son is treating his father as if he were already dead.[2] But in the father's gracious actions, he demonstrates a love that grants the younger son the freedom to reject and hurt him, and he gives in to the son's wishes.

One also has to realize that the father would be depending on those resources to support him in his old age. By giving in to the younger son, he is essentially risking his own well-being in his advancing years.[3] According to custom, even if the younger son had been given the father's property early, the father still should have had use of it. In turning his share into cash, the younger son is neglecting his responsibility to care for his parents.[4] By abandoning his father and leaving only the elder son to care for him, the younger son is further placing his father at risk, since it was important for parents to have children to take care of them as they grew older.[5] It was a deeply ingrained value in that culture to respect one's parents, and Deuteronomy 21:18–21 even says that rebellious children should be stoned.[6]

It does not seem to have taken long for the younger son to spend everything, and he soon finds himself in a precarious situation.

---

2. Kenneth E. Bailey, *Poet & Peasant and Through Peasant Eyes*, combined ed. (Grand Rapids: Eerdmans, 1983), 161–65.

3. Bailey, *Poet & Peasant*, 166. The Jewish text Sirach says that it is foolish for one to give one's property to one's children while one is still alive (Sirach 33:20–22).

4. David Wenham, *The Parables of Jesus* (Downers Grove, IL: InterVarsity, 1989), 106. *This is seen in the command to honor one's parents in Exod 20:12; Deut 5:16.*

5. Stephen Wright, *Tales Jesus Told: An Introduction to the Narrative Parables of Jesus* (Carlisle, UK: Paternoster, 2002), 56–57; Brad H. Young, *The Parables: Jewish Tradition and Christian Interpretation* (Grand Rapids: Baker, 1998), 144; Arland J. Hultgren, *The Parables of Jesus* (Grand Rapids: Eerdmans, 2000), 77.

6. "If someone has a stubborn and rebellious son who does not obey his father and mother and will not listen to them when they discipline him, his father and mother shall take hold of him and bring him to the elders at the gate of his town. They shall say to the elders, 'This son of ours is stubborn and rebellious. He will not obey us. He is a glutton and a drunkard.' Then all the men of his town are to stone him to death. You must purge the evil from among you. All Israel will hear of it and be afraid."

Famines were common in that time.[7] The son is in such dire need that he is in danger of starving. He finds work feeding pigs, which is yet another indication of how far he has fallen. To Jews, pigs were considered unclean (Lev 11:7; Deut 14:8; Isa 65:4; 66:17). Not only must he feed them, but he is so desperate that he wishes he could eat what the pigs are eating.[8]

At this point, the son decides he cannot go on and takes the risk to return home. His situation is so dire that he realizes he is worse off than his father's hired men. These men are the *misthoi*, hired in the morning to work throughout the day. They are day laborers without any assurance of ongoing work. They are considered lower on the social scale than indentured servants and even slaves, who would still have some security for their work and welfare.[9]

The son's situation is bleak indeed, and not simply because of his physical needs. Returning home had its own hazards. It would have been expected in that culture for the father to severely discipline or completely reject the younger son for his behavior. The son realizes that he can have no expectations of his father since he has forfeited his rights as a son.[10] He only hopes to be allowed to work as his servant.

But when the son returns, the father's welcome is nothing short of astonishing. As soon as he sees him, even though the son is still far off, he runs to meet him. Far from demonstrating any hesitation in accepting his wayward son, the father joyfully and enthusiastically runs to him, even before he knows why he has returned or what his motives are. He is overwhelmed with joy to have him home again.

---

7. For example, we read in Acts 11:27–30 that the prophet Agabus predicted a severe famine would hit the entire Roman Empire during the reign of Emperor Claudius.

8. The pods the pigs were eating were likely carob pods from evergreen trees. They were widely known as feed for animals and "food of desperation for humans." See Snodgrass, *Stories with Intent*, 126.

9. Hultgren, *Parables of Jesus*, 76–77.

10. Bernard Brandon Scott, *Hear Then the Parable* (Minneapolis: Fortress, 1989), 116.

The nature of the father's actions is more astounding considering that as the head of a Middle Eastern estate, running to greet the son would have been considered undignified and disgraceful.[11] In his culture, a man demonstrated who he was by the way he carried himself in public. As the Jewish document Sirach says, "A man's manner of walking tells you what he is" (Sirach 9:30).[12] But the father is so overcome with joy at his son's return that he cares more about being with his son than acting with proper decorum. The immediate commands for such an extravagant outpouring of affection and celebration would also have been startling. These details "illustrate God's amazing patience and love for his ungrateful children."[13]

The typical sequence would be for the son to fall down on his knees and request forgiveness. If the father granted this, there would be a set of expectations, and the son would essentially be on probation. There was no certainty he would be allowed to remain.[14] Here, though, the father accepts him without reservation. Despite the grave offense, he not only allows him to return, but overwhelmingly and joyfully receives him. He embraces and kisses him, the kiss being a sign of forgiveness and reconciliation.[15] The "best robe" that he orders the servants to put on him is likely the father's own robe that he would wear

---

11. Craig L. Blomberg, *Interpreting the Parables* (Downers Grove, IL: InterVarsity, 1990), 176.

12. Sirach is a book in what is known as the Old Testament Apocrypha, which is a collection of Jewish writings from the Second Temple period that are not included in the Christian canon. The Second Temple period is generally seen as extending from the sixth century BC to the destruction of the temple in AD 70. Sirach was written in the early second century BC. For more on this and other Jewish literature, see Daniel M. Gurtner, "Noncanonical Jewish Writings," in *The World of the New Testament,* ed. Joel B. Green and Lee Martin MacDonald (Grand Rapids: Baker, 2013), 290–309; also James C. VanderKam, *An Introduction to Early Judaism* (Eerdmans: Grand Rapids, 2001), 53–117.

13. Blomberg, *Interpreting the Parables,* 176.

14. Hultgren, *Parables of Jesus,* 78.

15. Bailey, *Poet & Peasant,* 182.

on special occasions.[16] There is disagreement on the significance of the ring, but the picture overall is one of acceptance.[17] The sandals placed on his feet show that in the house he is a free man, not a servant, and indeed he is the master of the servants who put the sandals on him.[18]

All of the symbols show that the son has been accepted back as a son, despite all of his great sins. The father not only welcomes him personally, but, as in our previous parables of the lost sheep and the lost coin, he also shares his joy with others. The celebration demonstrates the magnitude of the father's acceptance and joy. Simply to have meat at all reflects the significance of the situation, since generally people ate meat only on special occasions.[19] The fatted calf would be enough to feed the whole community and would be far too much for a single family. If the meal were only for the family, the animal would more likely be a goat or a sheep. The fattened calf was usually reserved for large occasions, such as a family wedding.[20] One estimate is that such an animal would be able to feed over one hundred people.[21]

It is important to note that the banquet the father throws in honor of the son would also serve to tell others they should forgive and accept the son as well. There is no hesitation in the father's welcome, and he immediately wants to show that he is accepted back into the

---

16. Wenham, *Parables of Jesus*, 108.

17. Darrell L. Bock, *Luke 9:51–24:53, Baker Exegetical Commentary on the New Testament* (Grand Rapids: Baker, 1996), 1315. Some see a reference to the signet ring, which signified authority; see Frederick W. Danker, *Jesus and the New Age* (Philadelphia: Fortress, 1988), 277; Wenham, *Parables of Jesus*, 108. See, for example, Gen 41:41–42, "So Pharaoh said to Joseph, 'I hereby put you in charge of the whole land of Egypt.' Then Pharaoh took his signet ring from his finger and put it on Joseph's finger"; or Esth 3:10, "So the king took his signet ring from his finger and gave it to Haman son of Hammedatha, the Agagite, the enemy of the Jews."

18. Bailey, *Poet & Peasant*, 185.

19. John Nolland, *Luke 9:21–18:34, Word Biblical Commentary 35B* (Dallas: Word, 1993), 786.

20. Wenham, *Parables of Jesus*, 108.

21. Bailey, *Poet & Peasant*, 186–87.

family and to celebrate with the entire community. The village would have been scandalized and offended by the son's behavior, and would likely have taunted and perhaps even physically harmed him for the way he treated his father. However, the father's actions would protect him from the town's hostility and enable him to be restored to fellowship among them.[22]

One can't help but wonder what it would be like to be the younger son. What were his thoughts as he approached his father's home? Was he overcome with shame at his actions, sorrow at the hurt he must have caused his father, fear at what kind of reaction he would receive, both from his family and from his village? Did he have enormous regret over his actions, which, together with the shame he bore, would have kept him from coming back if he had not been so desperate?

And what would it have been like to receive his father's embrace? Perhaps he was confused, maybe astonished, at the unexpected reception. How could he have ever imagined that he would be welcomed back after all he had done, the way he had so completely cut ties with and insulted his father? How overwhelming would it have been to experience not only the acceptance, but also his father's fervent desire to restore their relationship, his simple and profound joy over his presence? After living in fear and destitution for so long, the son could find refuge in this place of safety and warmth. How could he not have been overcome by his father's incomprehensible generosity, which could break down the last remaining walls of his hardened heart?

---

22. Bailey, *Poet & Peasant*, 181.

THE FATHER'S GRACE
AND THE ELDER SON

The father's embrace stands in stark contrast to the response of the elder son. Far from sharing in his father's joy, he rebels against his father and refuses to forgive his brother. We do not always notice that the elder son has also gravely insulted his father, just in a different way.

From the very beginning, it would have been the elder son's role to be a mediator for a family dispute. He should have demanded that the younger son apologize and try to reconcile the two, but he abdicates this responsibility.[23] When the other son returns, his harsh feelings toward his brother are clear in his refusal to show grace, despite his father's example. He demonstrates his distance from the younger son, referring to him as "this son of yours," which essentially means he is disowning his brother.[24] The elder son's accusation that his brother spent his money on prostitutes is likely unfounded and an exaggeration.[25] It is an intentional insult to his wayward sibling, designating him as the rebellious son. When he tells his father that the younger son squandered "your property" rather than "his property," this is likely implying that in his irresponsibility he has wasted the father's property which he would have needed to be cared for in his old age.[26] Unlike the father, the elder son is not willing to forgive and receive the younger son back into the family.

The elder son also demonstrates his own rebellion against his father. When the father throws the banquet for the returning son, according to custom the older son would have had particular responsibilities. He should be welcoming the guests and making sure they are taken care of, as well as guiding the servants. In essence, he should serve as the chief

---

23. Young, *Parables*, 141.

24. Wenham, *Parables of Jesus*, 108; Young, *Parables*, 141.

25. Wenham, *Parables of Jesus*, 108.

26. Bailey, *Poet & Peasant*, 199.

steward for this major household event. But not only does he neglect these duties, he even refuses to go into the house. He profoundly insults his father by not participating in the banquet he is hosting.[27]

The list goes on. He does not address his father with a proper title, as the repentant younger son does. Instead, he begins his speech by saying, "Look!" The content of his speech is particularly revealing. He says to his father that he has been "slaving" for him. Why would he regard himself as a slave rather than a son?

It is easy to see that the younger son thought of his father in terms of money and how he could benefit him. But the elder son does as well. His complaint about the feast thrown on his brother's behalf shows that he considers it a judgment on what the son is worth rather than an expression of his father's joy. It has been estimated that the goat the elder son had wanted would be worth less than one-tenth of the cow in the younger son's celebration and would require much less care and feeding.[28] In other words, "He reflects the atmosphere of a labor dispute over wages."[29] While the younger son was disobedient in leaving home, the elder son was disobedient while remaining at home. His words reveal that, like his sibling, he considered his father in terms of how he could benefit him. His relationship was a transactional one, just like his brother's.

The elder brother could still claim to be obedient, but he was obedient in order to get what he desired. He did what was expected in order to gain what he thought he deserved through his hard work. The result was that he did what his father might have asked, but he had no affection toward him. He considered him more of a boss than a father. "The elder brother viewed his father as an employer who

---

27. Bailey, *Poet & Peasant*, 194–95.
28. Hultgren, *Parables of Jesus*, 81.
29. Bailey, *Poet & Peasant*, 197.

must be obeyed instead of a parent who must be loved."[30] Indeed, far from loving his father, he shows his contempt through his reaction to his father's grace toward the wayward son.

RELATING TO GRACE

Since this parable comes right after the parables of the lost sheep and the lost coin, the audience is still the Pharisees and teachers of the law, who are criticizing Jesus for eating with "sinners" and tax collectors (Luke 15:1–2). The parable is in one sense a continuation of the lessons of the earlier parables. Here, though, we learn more about the one who is lost, the prodigal son, who is like the "sinners" and tax collectors who are condemned by the Pharisees. Despite his initial rebellion, the son eventually faces his predicament and his sin against his father and returns home, into the father's welcome.

Do you feel like the younger son? Do you identify more with the tax collectors and sinners, who would have heard in Jesus' message an overwhelming invitation of acceptance and forgiveness? Or does the situation of the elder son resonate more with you? It can be excruciating to see so much attention and rewards given to those who have messed up and come back with their tails between their legs. Why should their sins not only be overlooked but rewarded?

We find a very clear challenge for the Pharisees and teachers of the law to see in themselves the example of the elder son. Always dutiful, always conscientious, they have followed the law and believed in their own righteousness. In so doing they have found themselves unable to extend mercy to those who most need and desire it.

What sets the sons apart is their relationship to grace. The younger son repents and confesses his unworthiness to his father and in the end is restored as a son to his father's household. But we do not see

---

30. Young, *Parables*, 141.

any sense of remorse or repentance by the elder brother. The parable simply ends with the father's plea. This is in many ways the climax of the parable. It leaves us hanging, for we do not know how the son responds to his father's entreaties. It is here that the parable confronts us most directly with our own decision. As one author describes, "Parables often lead the listener on a collision course with destiny. Each one who follows the path of the drama must make a decision. The listener is invited to step up onto the stage of the play and act out the final scene. In reality, the conflict could be resolved in two different ways. Everything depends on the final decision of the elder brother, i.e., the listener."[31]

Will the Pharisees overcome their resentment toward those who do not "deserve" God's mercy? Or will they cling to their self-righteousness and demand that love and grace be "earned"? From what we know in the rest of the Gospels, the Pharisees were not able to let go of their preconceived notions and humbly present themselves in brokenness before God. What will we do?

RECEIVING THE FATHER'S GRACE

The responses of both sons challenge us, but in different ways.

The father receives the younger son because he is "filled with compassion" for him. He is able to look past the insults and the rejection, embrace his son, and rejoice in his return.

The father has essentially said to the younger son, I am so incredibly happy that you have returned home that I want to pull out all the stops. I want to have a lavish celebration for the entire village and let them all know that you, my son, have returned, and my family is whole again. I don't care what you did to me and what you did while you were gone. I am simply overcome with joy that you have come

---

31. Young, *Parables*, 155.

back to me. His response to the younger son is not just gracious and kind—it is overwhelming.

Like the younger son, we so often wait until we are desperate, when we have nowhere else to go. It is interesting that when the younger son rehearses his speech to his father, he ends with his appeal to be treated like one of the hired servants. But when he actually speaks to his father, he ends with, "I am no longer worthy to be called your son" (Luke 15:21).[32] The last words we hear from the son are his confession of the significance of what he has done, as he places himself at the father's mercy.

For the elder son, we would expect the father to be angry at being treated so contemptuously by him. Perhaps he might only ignore him, but he could also punish him. In any case, we would not be surprised for him to express his displeasure toward his son.

But once again, the father allows his love for his son to outweigh any disappointment or anger. When the son refuses to enter the house, the father himself comes out to speak with him. He looks past the son's insults and approaches him in love. Whereas the son did not address him with a title, the father affectionately begins by calling him "my son." He assures him that his rights are still protected, by telling him "everything I have is yours" (Luke 15:31). By this he lets him know that he is not a hired servant, even less a slave, but an heir.[33] The story ends with the father's assurance that he will always be with him and a plea to celebrate with him because his lost brother has been found.

---

32. Scholars present various possible reasons for the difference. Bock summarizes the reasons as including: (1) he was interrupted by his father; (2) since his father greeted him with such compassion, to include the comment would be an insult; and (3) the son was disappointed he could not earn back his relationship with his father. The words he originally rehearses are, "I am no longer worthy to be called your son; make me like one of your hired servants" (Luke 15:19). See Bock, *Luke 9:51–24:53*, 1314. At any rate, the significance of ending his statement with his confession of his unworthiness is to focus on what he has done, in contrast to the father's generous mercy.

33. Bailey, *Poet & Peasant*, 201.

He does not criticize or discipline him for his insolence, but begs him to accept his brother and join his father in extending grace.

The elder son challenges us in our self-righteousness. As much as I don't want to admit it, I can see how it would be maddening to see lavish rewards given to those who have been lazy and selfish or worse. It makes me wonder, What are the particular hurdles for those who have already served and sacrificed for God? Who have tried to keep his commands?

I see that my very desire to do the "right" things could itself become the problem because I can look down on those who have chosen differently. We see how the righteous Pharisees were unable to extend grace to "sinners." But they were also unable to see the grace available to themselves. In other words, perhaps the biggest danger of my own righteousness is how it tempts me to live by works rather than grace. It is hard to say "I am unworthy" when I am desperately trying to prove my worth.

I have to admit that it feels safer to depend on myself rather than God. I know God provides, but I check my retirement fund incessantly. If I have a problem with someone at work, I immediately want to fix things. That feels much better than pondering what God wants to do in my own heart so I can see what I did that led to the rift. I feel like Abraham with Hagar, unwilling to wait and trust and instead more than willing to give God a hand to make sure things work out (Gen 16).

What I don't realize is that I do this to protect myself because I am afraid of being caught short, or looking like a failure, or not getting what I want. I do this because what I really care about is myself. However, this hurts my ability to receive the truly good things God can give me. The Pharisees wanted control. What they lost was the opportunity to see and gain for themselves the good things God promises (Jas 1:17).

In order to receive grace we must, well, receive it. We must recognize it, know that we need it, and accept it. But to do this, we have to give up our delusion of perfection and self-sufficiency. We must also be willing to trust that God knows what he is doing.

When we focus on doing things our way, we may be tempted to treat God like a banker as the sons do, seeing him only as someone who can meet our desires and needs. The parable presents God as a loving father who provides his children with what they really need. And when his children stray, we are challenged to respond by accepting his compassion and forgiveness. However, God does not force us to respond. He merely presents and allows us to accept or reject him.

CONCLUSION: THE CHOICE TO RECEIVE

Although each son rejects the father in a different way, they are ultimately alike in their need for a real relationship with their father, not one based on calculation and gain. Both are sinners in a different way: one blatantly rejects his father and his ways, while the other cloaks his sin in self-righteousness. Yet, they are similar in that the cause of their sin is a shattered relationship with their father.[34]

Each son, like each one of us, needs to remember the Father's great desire to gain us back. The Father not only is willing, but he also yearns for his children. There is a well-known prayer in Mozart's *Requiem* that reflects his passion for us: "Remember, merciful Jesus, that I am the cause of your journey." Jesus indeed journeyed for us, even as Paul says in Romans 5:8, "while we were still sinners." The details of the parable show us that no matter the extent of our offense against God, the grace that awaits us is always available and overwhelming.

Indeed, the story ends with the father pleading with the elder son while the younger has already recognized his need and returned to the father. The parable causes us to examine our view of God and grace,

---

34. Young, *Parables*, 157.

our view of ourselves, and our view of others who receive God's grace. God's grace is ready and available, and the question is, Will we accept or reject what the Father wants to give us?

MAJOR TAKEWAYS

1. The younger son's offense includes not simply his selfish request for the inheritance and the way he squandered his fortune, but also a grave insult to his father in taking the money early and leaving his father at risk in his old age.

2. The elder son also gravely disrespects his father. He reveals that he thinks of himself more as a hired servant, working for pay, than a loved son. He also insults his father in the way he responds to the younger son's return, ignoring his duties as the elder son in refusing to help his father with the celebration.

3. The father's grace is represented by his overwhelming joy and acceptance at the younger son's return. But we also see it with his continued generosity and appeal to the elder son.

4. As with the parables of the lost sheep and the lost coin, the Pharisees and sinners who heard the parable are challenged to see and accept the grace God provides. The sinners are like the younger son, who is accepted by the father when he returns. The Pharisees are like the elder son, who is resentful at the grace given to the prodigal son.

QUESTIONS

1. What was the younger brother's sin? Consider how the cultural context magnifies his offense against the father.

2. What was the older brother's sin? Consider how the cultural context magnifies his offense against the father.

3. What was the father's grace to the younger son, and how did it restore him?

4. What was the father's grace to the older son, and how could it restore him?

5. What would make it difficult for the older son to accept the father's grace? As you invite the Holy Spirit into your story, what makes it difficult for you to accept God's grace?

6. What challenges do you think the younger son would have faced in deciding to go back to his father? What challenges are you facing?

7. Which son do you identify with more? Why? What might it look like to ask God to help you accept his grace for yourself?

GENEROUS GRACE

*THE PARABLE OF THE
WORKERS IN THE VINEYARD
(MATTHEW 20:1–16)*

For the kingdom of heaven is like a landowner who went out early in the morning to hire workers for his vineyard. He agreed to pay them a denarius for the day and sent them into his vineyard.

About nine in the morning he went out and saw others standing in the marketplace doing nothing. He told them, "You also go and work in my vineyard, and I will pay you whatever is right." So they went.

He went out again about noon and about three in the afternoon and did the same thing. About five in the afternoon he went out and found still others standing around. He asked them, "Why have you been standing here all day long doing nothing?"

"Because no one has hired us," they answered.

He said to them, "You also go and work in my vineyard."

When evening came, the owner of the vineyard said to his foreman, "Call the workers and pay them their wages, beginning with the last ones hired and going on to the first."

The workers who were hired about five in the after-noon came and each received a denarius. So when those came who were hired first, they expected to receive more. But each one of them also received a denarius. When they received it, they began to grumble against the land-owner. "These who were hired last worked only one hour," they said, "and you have made them equal to us who have borne the burden of the work and the heat of the day."

But he answered one of them, "I am not being unfair to you, friend. Didn't you agree to work for a denarius? Take your pay and go. I want to give the one who was hired last the same as I gave you. Don't I have the right to do what I want with my own money? Or are you envious because I am generous?"

So the last will be first, and the first will be last.

INTRODUCTION

After I graduated from college, I took a job teaching fourth grade at a small Christian school. It so happened that was the year the school planned to take the teachers to Israel during the Christmas break. It was an exciting opportunity. The principal of the school thought that her instructors would be more equipped to teach the Bible if they had seen and experienced the Holy Land themselves.

As to be expected, the school would not automatically pay for everyone's trip. The amount the school paid would depend on how long each person had taught there. Since I had only started, my benefit would be $0. I could not afford to pay my own way, and so I expected to be left behind. I was a little disappointed, but knew it would not be fair to receive the same benefit as others who had already worked there for many years.

However, the principal offered to have the school pay my way if I agreed to teach for seven years (which reminded me a little of Jacob agreeing to work for Laban for seven years in order to marry Rachel!). It was a tempting offer, but since I was just out of college, I wasn't ready to make that long of a commitment. I politely turned the offer down, thinking that was the end of that. To my amazement, a few days later I received a letter telling me that the school would pay for my entire trip. No explanation, no expectations, just the gracious offer.

The trip to Israel, as you may imagine, was wonderful and life changing. We sailed on the Sea of Galilee, walked in Jerusalem, were baptized in the Jordan River. I will forever carry those images of being in the land where Jesus lived. But the trip had another effect on me. I was incredibly grateful for my principal's generosity. I knew I had received something precious I had not earned.

Jesus tells a parable about generosity and people who receive something they do not deserve. In the parable of the workers in the vineyard, some of the laborers earn pay that they have not worked for. However, to understand the intent of the parable, we need not just to know what the people receive or why they do not deserve it, but we also need to consider the generous giver. In other words, to understand grace, we begin not from our need and what we get, but from the perspective of the God who gives.

THE PARABLE

The setting of this fascinating parable is a typical scene in first-century Israel. Day laborers gather in the marketplace, hoping someone will offer them employment for the day. Their situation is dire. They are dependent on being hired since they do not own their own land. They do not even have the relative security of steady work that slaves have.[1] All they can do is wait to see whether someone needs their labor this day. It is critical that they are hired. If they are not, their family will go hungry.[2]

The landowner has his own concerns. The time is likely the harvest season for grapes, where additional hands are especially needed. It is urgent that he harvest the crop in a timely fashion. Precision is important. If the harvest is a day late, the landowner may lose the crop. But if he is one day too early, the crop may lose value in the marketplace.[3] For the landowner to make the most of his investment, he must hire the appropriate number of workers.

This is likely the situation behind the parable. What will the landowner do, and what will happen to the workers? The owner sets out at six a.m. to hire the people he needs, agreeing to pay the normal day's wage, a denarius. This was not a large amount of money for an entire day of backbreaking work in the scorching sun, but it would be enough to feed a family. In the third hour, nine a.m., the owner returns to hire more workers. He does not promise them a denarius, but rather says that he will pay them "whatever is right" (Matt 20:4). He does the same at noon, and three p.m.[4] He returns one final time at five p.m., the eleventh hour. Now, however, he does not say anything about pay, only telling the men, "You also go and work in my vineyard."[5]

---

1. As mentioned in the chapter on the prodigal son.

2. Brad H. Young, *The Parables: Jewish Tradition and Christian Interpretation* (Grand Rapids: Baker, 1998), 70.

3. Young, *Parables*, 70.

4. The workday was calculated by three-hour increments, beginning at 6 a.m. and ending at 6 p.m.

5. One question that naturally arises is, Why did the owner keep going back instead of hiring all of the workers he needed from the beginning? Various explanations have been proposed, for example, that if it had been a Friday, he would be in a hurry to finish before the Sabbath, or that some of the workers didn't show up until later. Since it is hard to determine, it may be best not to speculate at this point. Hultgren proposes that it may simply be that "the story has been composed with its ends in view," since it does not seem to correspond precisely to real life. See Arland J. Hultgren, *The Parables*

At the end of the day, he has the foreman bring the workers to pay them their wages. He instructs him to begin with the ones who were hired last. To the workers' amazement, he gives them a denarius, even though they only worked one hour. He continues with the others, until he gets to the ones who had been hired first. Having worked all day, they now expect to receive more than a denarius. But to their surprise and consternation, they receive the same as the last-hired workers. At this they complain to the owner that he has made them "equal" to the ones who worked only one hour when they toiled all day in the hot sun (Matt 20:12).

The owner responds that he has not been unfair since he paid them what they had all agreed to from the beginning. He has the right to do what he wants with his money. He ends by pointing out that the problem may be that they are envious because of his generosity.

RESPONDING TO THE PARABLE: THE IMPORTANCE OF THE ENDING

The parable challenges us to discover our hearts as we consider our own response to the generous landowner. Are we upset that the latecomers received the same reward as the ones who were there all day, or are we glad that the owner was generous since this meant everyone would be able to feed their families? Do we relate with the workers who worked all day without a greater reward or the ones who only worked an hour and received the same benefit? What do we think about the owner's comment to the ones who complained?

The owner's actions are shocking when we consider the normal practice of the time. The men who complain would be justified in seeing a big problem with what he has done. If anything, the owner's words are harsh. In their minds, the others get a reward they did not

---

of Jesus (Grand Rapids: Eerdmans, 2000), 37.

earn, while they get a scolding from the master after laboring hard all day!

The parable focuses on the response of the ones who worked all day. We see this even in the way the final scene is set up. The owner specifically tells the steward the order for paying the workers. The expected order would be to start with the ones who had worked all day. If he had done this, they would not have seen what the others received and so would not have been disgruntled at getting the same amount. Each of the other groups would then have been surprised and delighted to get the same amount. Everyone would have left happy and pleased, and the landowner would have avoided the heated confrontation. However, he specifically reversed the order, which indicates that he purposely wanted those who worked all day to see the grace he would give to those who had not worked as long.[6]

We don't know how the first hired workers responded to the owner's rebuke. Perhaps after the owner's rebuke, they changed their perspective and rejoiced in the good fortune of the others. Or perhaps they continued to grumble to the owner. Since Jesus does not tell us how they responded, we are invited to imagine ourselves in the story and apply the conclusion to our own lives. How would we respond to the owner, and what does that tell us about ourselves?

RESPONDING TO THE PARABLE: GOD, JUSTICE, AND GENEROSITY

As we consider our response to the landowner, it is good to notice that Jesus begins the parable by saying "The kingdom of heaven is like ..." In other words, he tells us what we can expect in a kingdom that is ruled by God. The owner's treatment of the workers who were hired

---

6. Kenneth E. Bailey, *Jesus through Middle Eastern Eyes: Cultural Studies in the Gospels* (Downers Grove, IL: IVP Academic, 2008), 360. For these workers, their employment is particularly precarious since it is seasonal (Hultgren, *Parables of Jesus*, 36).

later shows us that God rules his kingdom with amazing generosity. Looking at the parable from the standpoint of the owner can radically change what we get out of the parable. The point is not that the first workers are underpaid. The point is that the others are *overpaid*. The owner gives them more than they expect and deserve.

Sadly, though, the first workers are not able to see this because they are focused on what they believe to be fair. Why should they get the same as the ones who did not work as hard? They are upset at the grace shown to the others, and this colors their response. Instead of seeing the beauty of grace, they focus on injustice. As a result, instead of being grateful, they become bitter. As one writer puts it, "Grace is not only amazing, it is also—for certain types—*infuriating!*"[7]

How does the grace of God conflict with our ideas of justice? I think of how much I want things to be just. If I work hard, I want it to be rewarded. If I do something good, I want to be recognized for it. If I sacrifice for someone, I want them to notice it. The problem is, I don't see the flip side. How often do I need forgiveness for a mean-spirited word, for failing to take care of a problem adequately, for neglecting to do something I should have done a long time ago? I wonder how things would turn out if I were to add up all of my "good deeds" and subtract all of my offenses. I'm pretty sure I don't want to know.

So I probably don't want to be too hard on the first workers because I see a lot of myself in them. I suspect that most of us do. The parable challenges us to confront our own sense of self-righteousness and justice and instead to trust in the justice of God's grace, which is characterized by generous mercy. By allowing the parable to confront me, I may have a different perspective on my own sense of justice. Perhaps I feel wronged in relation to others, but it is nothing in comparison to what I have received from God.

---

7. Bailey, *Jesus through Middle Eastern Eyes*, 361.

The parable can prod us forward as we consider our situations from the standpoint of God's justice and grace. Consider how the landowner answers the disgruntled workers. He does not respond to the accusation directly, but rather redirects the issue. The owner's response to the complaining workers is, "I am not being unfair to you. … Don't I have the right to do what I want with my own money? Or are you envious because I am generous?" God is not unfair. He is generous.

It is crucial to see that while the workers see it as an issue of unfairness, the owner reframes it from the perspective of generosity.[8] The workers see a wrong done to them. He wants them to see the benefit of receiving from a gracious benefactor.

We may be saved by grace, but it is amazingly easy to fall into the trap of wanting to be rewarded for our works and envying those who get even though they don't seem to give. But how can anything we do compare to what God has done for us? In other words, we are like the Pharisees in the parable of the prodigal son. Like the Pharisees, we can close the door to seeing how God might bless us with his overwhelming generosity. The first workers were unable to see this possibility for themselves, because they were too busy complaining over their unfair treatment. They were focused on the perceived injustice rather than realizing that they worked for a kind and merciful employer.

Because really, aren't we all the eleventh-hour workers? We have all been saved by grace and received more than we deserve. The point of the parable may be to confront those of us who neglect grace and the gracious giver. We may think we want just rewards when we would be much better off simply receiving from the one whose mercy and generosity are unending. In wanting God to withhold from those we don't think "deserve" it as much as we do, we close ourselves off to his grace.

---

8. Hultgren, *Parables of Jesus*, 39.

RESPONDING TO THE PARABLE: GOD'S GOODNESS

It is interesting to note that right before this parable we have the story of the rich young ruler (Matt 19:16–22).[9] In this story, the rich young ruler approaches Jesus, asking what he must do to gain eternal life. Jesus responds that he must obey God's commandments, to which the man replies that he has done this. He then asks what else he must do. Jesus challenges him to sell all of his possessions, give to the poor, and follow him if he wants to have treasure in heaven. At this, the young man sadly walks away.

Jesus then explains to his disciples that it is virtually impossible, from a human standpoint, for those who have wealth to enter the kingdom of God (Matt 19:23–30). Since prosperity was viewed as a sign of divine blessing and favor, this would be shocking to his first-century audience.[10] Who could be saved if not the rich? This encounter prompts Peter to ask Jesus who can then be saved. Jesus responds this is only possible through God.

Peter then mentions that the disciples have given up "everything" to follow Jesus and seek the kingdom of heaven, and he asks, "What then will there be for us?" (Matt 19:27). What a fascinating and human response this is! After Jesus says only God can save, Peter seems to assume that God will do this as a reward in response to their sacrifice.

It seems fitting that the parable steers us to consider that rather than focusing on rewards, we should trust a gracious and generous

---

9. In Luke's version of the story, he calls him a "ruler" (Luke 18:18). Most likely he was some type of religious lay leader. It is possible that he was a Pharisee (Michael J. Wilkins, *Matthew, NIV Application Commentary* [Grand Rapids: Zondervan, 2004], 647).

10. For example, Ps 112:1, 3 states, "Blessed are those who fear the LORD, who find great delight in his commands. ... Wealth and riches are in their houses, and their righteousness endures forever." Deuteronomy 28:11 says that God will grant "abundant prosperity" to those who keep his commands.

Father. As one author puts it, "Christ was saying that disciples are to fulfill the work entrusted to them, leaving the distribution of the reward to Him. The Lord is just, gracious, and generous; and He will do what is right."[11] This challenges us to consider our ideas about God. Do we judge God by our own ideas of what is fair and just, or do we trust that he will give us good things and all that we need?[12]

Even the hiring of the workers may reflect the kindness of God. The owner would not normally be the one to hire the workers. That would be the job of the steward, who was tasked with managing the estate. Furthermore, we see that the owner goes to the marketplace and back not once but five times to hire the workers, and in the heat of the day. Indeed, the steward does not appear until the end of the story, when it is time to pay the workers.[13] The owner is not a distant lord, but is intimately involved in the affairs of his work force, and his involvement is one of caring and grace.

Do we see that grace, or like the workers, do we use the lens of comparison and competition to think we deserve more? It's interesting how we can be content with something until we see what someone else has. It's not that our own situation has changed. We just become discontented because we are jealous of what someone else has.

A few years ago my colleagues and I moved into a beautiful new building on campus. I was thrilled that my new office had a big window with a nice view of the central courtyard. My previous office had been a nice but windowless room underneath the chapel. With our offices basically underground and being in southern California, we would

---

11. J. Dwight Pentecost, *The Parables of Jesus* (Grand Rapids: Zondervan, 1982), 124.

12. There is the question as to what is meant by passages such as Rom 8:28 and God's providing for the believer's "good." This is an important question that will be covered in the chapter on the parable of the friend at midnight.

13. Bailey describes such actions as "unheard of" (*Jesus through Middle Eastern Eyes*, 360–63).

semi-joke that we would rather not be in our offices when the next earthquake hit.

Now, with my brand-new office letting in the beautiful southern California sunniness, I was very happy, until … I saw the view someone else had. Her office was on the other side of the hallway, and she was able to see the snow-capped mountains off in the distance. Suddenly, my view didn't seem so nice at all. Instead of being grateful for the window, I became unhappy that my window looked straight out onto a bunch of buildings. I was no longer content just to have a window because I saw that someone had something better.

Comparison can also injure our relationships with others, as we have seen. When we compare what we have or have done, we can become self-righteous because we think we deserve more, which means that, well, we think we are more deserving. We end up with a higher view of ourselves, which then translates into a lesser view of others. This certainly doesn't fit well with Paul's command to "in humility value others above yourselves" (Phil 2:3).

But to think this way goes against human nature. Psychologists have found that many people would turn down money if they thought that someone else is getting more. In one experiment people were offered a small amount of money ($2), but with the catch that another person would get a larger sum ($8). An overwhelming amount of people—85 percent—declined the offer. They would rather receive nothing than have someone else get more than they got.

Similar studies produced the same results, sometimes using larger hypothetical amounts of money. What does all this research indicate? We are strongly oriented toward justice, and comparisons with other people matter *a lot*. We don't just think about how we are doing. We think about how we are doing compared with everyone else, and that affects how we act.[14]

But while we are wired for fairness, grace is what transforms and heals. We think differently when we focus on God's grace. Can you imagine what the last-hired workers thought? Each passing hour would have increased their dread in having to go home to tell their families that they had failed to provide and everyone would go hungry. Instead, though, they realized that they wouldn't have to do this, that their families would have enough, even though they knew they didn't deserve it. I suspect they would have been overjoyed at their good fortune, profoundly relieved, and extraordinarily grateful.

I imagine what it would have been like for both sets of workers to go home. Both had the same reward, enough to feed their families. But the first ones would have gone home unhappy, perhaps spending the rest of the night grumbling about those who didn't deserve what they got. Did they wake up the next morning, still unhappy about a world that is unfair, continuing to complain to anyone who would listen? Would the last workers have woken up hopeful, knowing that even in an unfair world, God is still good, and so wanting to do good to others? One writer describes the reaction of the person who can appreciate the grace given: "The person who has received the mercy of forgiveness of God will have the deepest sense of thankfulness for the new life he or she has received and in turn will extend mercy and forgiveness to others as a natural response."[15] How can we better understand and accept the mercy and forgiveness of God?

---

14. Nathan A. Heflick, "Wanting Less, So Long as Others Don't Get More," *Psychology Today*, March 31, 2017, https://www.psychologytoday.com/us/blog/the-big-questions/201703/wanting-less-so-long-others-dont-get-more.

15. Wilkins, *Matthew*, 675.

CONCLUSION: THE GENEROSITY
OF GOD'S GRACE

To be truly transformative, grace must be deeply received. *Les Misérables* is a classic book that many people have either read or more likely seen the play or movie based on the book. A critical scene is when the hero, Jean Valjean, has just been released from a nineteenth-century French prison. People do not want to help an ex-convict, and only the bishop of Digne offers him food and shelter. Later that night Valjean pays back the man's kindness by beating and robbing him. However, when the police catch him and he is about to be sent back to jail, the priest gives him grace. Rather than seeking justice or even revenge for Valjean's betrayal, he tells the police that he gave Valjean the stolen goods, so they have to release him. And if that weren't enough, the priest even gives him some precious silver candlesticks to sell in order to start a new life.

The moment marks a turning point in Valjean's life. When he realizes that grace—abundant grace—is available to him, he responds by becoming a person who gives grace to others. It is a beautiful story, and yet every time I think of the scene, I can't help but wonder, What if he had not recognized and appreciated the grace that had been given to him? What if he had simply taken the goods, laughed at the priest for being naive, and continued on to a life of crime and violence? One could say he still received grace since he did not go to prison. But did he really? The power of grace lies not just in the giving but also in the receiving—that is, realizing that mercy and generosity are meaningful and transforming and allowing oneself to be the recipient of what is abundantly given by another.

Because of the central role of the owner, some have proposed that the parable of the workers in the vineyard might be better called something like the parable of the generous employer. This may be a more accurate title that would also help us in our response. After all, is the point the workers and their situation, or the employer and his generosity? I think God presents us with grace every day in ways we too often neither see nor appreciate. Grace is intended to change us, to make us more like the one who is the primary grace-giver, and the Holy Spirit can open our eyes to see it and our hearts to receive it. When grace appears, we can respond. We can complain about God's fairness or rejoice that we serve a generous and merciful God.

MAJOR TAKEAWAYS

1. The focus of the parable is ultimately on the generous landowner.
2. The response of the workers helps us consider our own responses to God's generosity. Do we rejoice in his grace to the last-hired workers or dwell on the unfairness to the ones who worked all day but did not receive more compensation?
3. The context of the parable in Matthew's Gospel reveals that Jesus is warning against doing kingdom work for the sake of rewards.
4. The parable illustrates the importance of receiving grace as compared with demanding justice. Receiving grace produces a humble and grateful soul that in turn extends grace to others. Demanding justice can lead to a bitter and discontented soul and hinder our ability to see the needs of others.
5. The parable challenges us to consider the way we view God: according to our own standards of justice, or trusting that he will provide what is good.

QUESTIONS

1. Pretend you are one of the workers who has labored all day under the scorching sun. You expectantly approach the owner anticipating a great reward, but receive the same amount as those who stood around all day and only worked one hour! What is your reaction, and why?

2. Pretend you are the one of the workers who waited most of the day, were hired at the last minute, and expected to be paid only a portion of a day's work. You dread going home with only a fraction of what your family needs. But now the owner gives you a full day's pay. How do you react, and why?

3. Which set of workers do you identify with most, and why?

4. Think of a time when you did not get what you expected or thought you deserved. How did you react, and why?

5. Think of a time when you received grace and how you responded. How might this make you want to extend grace to others?

6. Ask the Holy Spirit to impress on your heart an area in which you are focused on justice and less able to see grace. How can he change the way you consider the situation as you think about God's incredible grace to you?

TRANSFORMING GRACE

When one of the Pharisees invited Jesus to have dinner with him, he went to the Pharisee's house and reclined at the table. A woman in that town who lived a sinful life learned that Jesus was eating at the Pharisee's house, so she came there with an alabaster jar of perfume. As she stood behind him at his feet weeping, she began to wet his feet with her tears. Then she wiped them with her hair, kissed them and poured perfume on them.

When the Pharisee who had invited him saw this, he said to himself, "If this man were a prophet, he would know who is touching him and what kind of woman she is—that she is a sinner."

Jesus answered him, "Simon, I have something to tell you."

"Tell me, teacher," he said.

"Two people owed money to a certain moneylender. One owed him five hundred denarii, and the other fifty. Neither of them had the money to pay him back, so he *forgave the debts of both. Now which of them will love him more?"*

Simon replied, "I suppose the one who had the bigger debt forgiven."

"You have judged correctly," Jesus said.

Then he turned toward the woman and said to Simon, "Do you see this woman? I came into your house. You did not give me any water for my feet, but she wet my feet with her tears and wiped them with her hair. You did not give me a kiss, but this woman, from the time I entered, has not stopped kissing my feet. You did not put oil on my head, but she has poured perfume on my feet. Therefore, I tell you, her many sins have been forgiven—as her great love has shown. But whoever has been forgiven little loves little."

Then Jesus said to her, "Your sins are forgiven."

The other guests began to say among themselves, "Who is this who even forgives sins?"

Jesus said to the woman, "Your faith has saved you; go in peace."

INTRODUCTION

There is a fairly well-known optical illusion known as "The Young Lady or an Old Hag?" Depending on how you look at the picture, you can either see a lovely young woman or an aged, withered woman. The amazing thing is that both are actually there. What you see just depends on what you focus on.

Our perspective on a situation can change once we get new information or learn to see something in another way. For example, think of the parent who is worried sick when their child misses curfew, until they learn that the child has been at a classmate's house the whole time and just forgot to call.

Jesus used parables to challenge people to look at the kingdom in new ways. The parables do not just inform, but also challenge us to change our perspective on what the kingdom is like, why it is important, and how we can respond. But to do this, they may also compel us to face uncomfortable truths about ourselves. In the parable of the two debtors, we are invited to look with two pairs of eyes at a sinful woman. With one pair, we see a person who should be rejected and shunned. With another pair of eyes, the eyes of grace, we see a person loved and saved by Jesus, who shows us how to respond to Jesus' compassion with a heart overflowing with gratitude.

THE PARABLE

Jesus relates the brief parable in an interaction with Simon the Pharisee. The whole story begins with Simon's invitation for Jesus to dine with him at his home. There could have been various occasions for this. One possibility is that Jesus had been preaching in the local synagogue, after which the Pharisee had invited him over for the Sabbath meal.[1] Others have proposed the meal is patterned after the Greek *symposia,* which were drinking parties that followed a banquet and were characterized by lively conversation and perhaps even debate.[2] Whatever the occasion, there would have been certain expectations for hospitality from Simon as the host. As a Pharisee, he would also have been obligated to maintain certain conventions of ritual purity.[3]

---

1. Simon J. Kistemaker, *The Parables: Understanding the Stories Jesus Told* (Grand Rapids: Baker, 1980), 136.

2. Joel B. Green, *The Gospel of Luke,* New International Commentary on the New Testament (Grand Rapids: Eerdmans, 1997), 306.

3. As Bailey describes, "Isolation from impure food and people was especially crucial for the Pharisee when he sat down to eat. Jesus enters into this kind of a world when he accepts the invitation." Kenneth E. Bailey, *Poet & Peasant and Through Peasant*

At some point during the meal, a woman who is known to have lived a sinful life enters. As she stands behind Jesus, weeping, she wets his feet with her tears and then wipes them with her hair, kisses them, and pours perfume on them.

Simon is shocked that Jesus is allowing this. Although he respectfully addresses him with the title "teacher" (Luke 7:40), Jesus' actions cause Simon to doubt him. He thinks that if Jesus were really a prophet, he would know "who and what sort of woman" was touching him, with the implication that he would not allow that to happen. In response, Jesus tells the parable of the two debtors.[4]

The parable itself is quite simple. Two men owe money to a moneylender. One has a large debt—five hundred denarii, or about a year-and-a-half's wages.[5] The other's debt is substantially smaller, only fifty denarii. Both have their debts canceled. Jesus' question is straightforward: Given how much each has been forgiven, who will love the moneylender more?

Simon would have been familiar with the Roman customs concerning debt and obligation. However, Jesus turns the ancient system upside down by saying the woman's action should not be understood as repaying a debt as much as coming from love that results from having the debts canceled.[6]

Eyes, combined ed. (Grand Rapids: Eerdmans, 1983), 3.

4. Interestingly, even though Simon thinks Jesus has invalidated any claim to being a prophet, Jesus shows that he actually is a prophet by responding to him even though Simon only spoke his objection to himself (Green, *Gospel of Luke*, 311).

5. The denarius was considered a normal wage for a day laborer. This would assume a person worked about three hundred days a year.

6. It seems likely that Simon is relatively wealthy, since he is hosting a formal banquet. Although not all Pharisees were rich, they are referred to as those "who loved money" in Luke 16:14, and what happens in this story seems to fit with a general characterization of them as those who placed a high priority on status and privilege (Green, *Gospel of Luke*, 311n97).

Simon answers Jesus' question about which debtor will love the creditor more by saying "the one who had the bigger debt forgiven." Jesus tells him he is correct and then applies the lesson of the parable. In contrast to the lavish display of the woman, Simon did not offer him any water to wash his feet or give him a kiss. It is not certain how much would have been required of a host. But whatever the case, Luke clearly shows us Jesus considers what the woman does extraordinary, demonstrating great love and devotion.

Jesus says her sins have been forgiven "as her great love has shown." Then, in what would be an allusion to Simon, he also gives the flip side, saying, "Whoever has been forgiven little loves little" (Luke 7:47).

FINDING THE "TWIST"
IN THE PARABLE

On the one hand, Jesus' parable and lesson seem straightforward. The woman loves much because she has been forgiven much. The larger the burden lifted, the greater the gratitude. Great sin does not mean one is hopelessly lost, but provides an opportunity for God to demonstrate his abundant grace. One who knows how much one has received loves God in response to what one has been forgiven.

The proposition makes sense. After all, we see Paul's great devotion to Christ even though he considered himself to have been the "worst" of sinners (1 Tim 1:15). But the story also presents a potential problem: Does one need to sin much in order to love much? Or to put it another way, if one has been "good" and only sins a little, can that person never have great love for Jesus?

I like to tease my students with this thought. Isn't this a great parable? I tell them. Look at the grace that Jesus gives this woman, someone who was probably shunned and humiliated by everyone else around her. Jesus affirms her in front of everyone and removes her shame. In the classroom, many heads nod. I continue. We want to love Jesus a lot, right? Yes, they readily agree. Well, then according to this parable, we love Jesus the more we've been forgiven. But in order to be forgiven a lot, what do we need to do first? Silence. Some students squirm in their chairs. Mostly their faces break into wide grins, and there is muffled laughter.

Finally someone speaks. We need to sin a lot, says the student. Yes, that's it! I respond. I feign as much enthusiasm as I can. We finally have the answer! Since we want to love Jesus a lot, we need to sin more! Take the whole weekend and sin as much as you can! The more you can sin, the more you'll love Jesus! Just remember to ask for forgiveness. Isn't this great?

By this point, the students can see what I am doing and start to protest. So we talk about the parable. What could Jesus mean? The answer, I tell them, lies in recognizing how this would be heard by Simon the Pharisee.

SIMON'S RESPONSE

In many ways, Simon's response to the woman would not have been surprising in the cultural context. Her presence would have been automatically objectionable, particularly for a Pharisee such as he. That she is described as someone known in the town as a sinner "marks her as a prostitute by vocation, a whore by social status, contagious in her impurity."[7] As a Pharisee, Simon would have had a great concern

---

7. Green, *Gospel of Luke*, 309. One question is how she would have gained entrance to the meal in the first place. Many have noted this could be the result of the open nature of Palestinian homes, and perhaps even the custom of allowing others to observe a meal. Pentecost notes, "For such an occasion as this a Pharisee would set the table in an open place, perhaps in the courtyard. The host would leave open the front gate so that passers-by might not only observe the hospitality of the host, but even enter the courtyard to view the food that the host has provided for the guests." See J. Dwight Pentecost, *The Parables of Jesus* (Grand Rapids: Zondervan, 1982), 32. But as Green notes, this does not resolve the basic problem of purity and holiness that her presence would have created (*Gospel of Luke*, 309).

for purity at meals. Jesus' lack of concern over defilement is sufficient proof that Jesus is not a prophet, for a prophet would know who she was and not allow himself to have contact with someone like her.[8]

The nature of her actions could cause even more objections. The formal dining area was called a *triclinium,* in which people would recline on couches in a U-shaped formation. The diners would recline on their left sides, eating with their right hands from a table in front of them. Their legs would either be tucked behind them or stretched out behind the person next to them.[9] This would allow the woman to come "behind" (Luke 7:38) to gain access to his feet. If the woman was a prostitute, and also because women in general were often seen as temptresses, Simon would easily have viewed her actions as being erotic in nature.[10] Letting her hair down would only increase this perception. It was considered a disgrace for a woman to unbind her hair in public, and maybe even grounds for divorce.[11] One commentator describes this as the same today as being topless in public.[12]

The question, though, is whether Simon will see what is truly happening in front of him. The woman's actions are compelled by her gratitude for the forgiveness she has received. Her actions are extravagant, far beyond what is necessary. She washes Jesus' feet, an action

---

8. Simon's condemnation of Jesus over his contact with the woman, similar to the other Pharisees' objections over Jesus' association with sinners, is an attitude seen in other early Jewish literature. For example, "So no one pities a person who associates with a sinner and becomes involved in the other's sins" (Sirach 12:14); "What does a wolf have in common with a lamb? No more has a sinner with the devout" (Sirach 13:17).

9. David Wenham, *The Parables of Jesus* (Downers Grove, IL: InterVarsity, 1989), 96; Green, *Gospel of Luke,* 310.

10. Not all scholars think the woman was a prostitute. As Bock notes, "The exact basis for the woman's description as a sinner is unknown." Darrell L. Bock, *Luke 1:1–9:50, Baker Exegetical Commentary on the New Testament* (Grand Rapids: Baker, 1994), 695.

11. Wenham, *Parables of Jesus,* 98.

12. Green, *Gospel of Luke,* 310.

normally reserved for slaves, and she does this not with water, but with her own tears. She kisses his feet and pours perfume on them. All these actions are especially significant since feet were the dirtiest part of the body and so the subject of the lowliest tasks.[13] Nevertheless, she is so overwhelmed with gratitude that she has lost her sense of self-consciousness and freely does what is considered disgraceful in the eyes of other people.[14]

However, Simon continues to see her as a sinner, and so one to be turned away. This forms the basis of his complaint against Jesus. If Jesus were truly a prophet, "he would know who is touching him and what kind of woman she is—that she is a sinner" (Luke 7:39). He cannot see what has happened to her and be moved by her enormous gratitude. Instead, he accuses Jesus of being spiritually blind for allowing her to touch him.[15]

It would be apparent to Simon and everyone else that he, as the righteous Pharisee, is being equated with the debtor who was forgiven little and therefore loves little. But we might need to ask the question, Does Simon *really* need to be forgiven just a "little"?

Throughout Luke's Gospel, as well as the rest of the Gospels, we see how the Pharisees continually rejected Jesus and his mission, being unable to see what Jesus was truly doing. In Luke's Gospel, they are not typically seen as righteous, but "full of greed and wickedness" (Luke 11:39). They may think they are righteous, but Jesus has a different opinion of them.

It seems that the incident with Simon is a prime example of how the Pharisees missed what God was doing through Jesus. Simon exemplifies how the Pharisees focused on the law while neglecting God's

---

13. Wenham, *Parables of Jesus*, 98.

14. Brad H. Young, *The Parables: Jewish Tradition and Christian Interpretation* (*Grand Rapids: Baker, 1998*), 165.

15. Wenham, *Parables of Jesus*, 98.

love. Jesus condemns them for following the letter of the law while neglecting "justice and the love of God" (Luke 11:42). Simon cannot get beyond the woman's past. Jesus sees her repentance from her past and acceptance of grace.

Perhaps even more so, Simon also cannot see himself correctly. Clearly the woman has sinned much, but she has recognized her fallenness and received grace, resulting in her great love toward Jesus. Simon has sinned greatly in his judgment of Jesus and the woman, failing to open his heart and mind to see what God is doing. What Jesus reveals in his rebuke of Simon are his internal sins of "pride, arrogance, hard-heartedness, hostility, a judgmental spirit, slim understanding of what really defiles."[16]

Simon focuses on the external part of the law and sees himself as righteous. He does not realize that in terms of sins of the heart, he is in great need of forgiveness. As a result, since he does not see himself in need of grace, he receives little forgiveness. Therefore, he loves little because he has been forgiven little, even though God's abundant grace would be available to him as well.

RESPONDING TO THE PARABLE

In the letter to the Romans, Paul teaches us that "all have sinned and fall short of the glory of God" (Rom 3:23). The woman responds to Jesus' message and is overwhelmed with gratitude at the magnitude of the gift she has been given. Perhaps she recognizes—more deeply and profoundly than the rest of us—how our sinful hearts stand in desperate need of forgiveness.

If the parable points to the response, then it is likely no coincidence that we do not know Simon's response. Luke leaves us hanging. Will Simon be like the other Pharisees and continue to reject God's

---

16. Bailey, *Through Peasant Eyes*, 18.

salvation? Or will he see the true state of his heart and humble himself, like the sinful woman, and receive the grace Jesus offers? As Luke does not give us Simon's response, we as the audience are left to evaluate our own responses. Will we harden our hearts as we consider our own "righteousness," or will we recognize our need for God's mercy in light of our great sin? Will we open our hearts to being transformed by God's grace so that the abundance of what God has given us flows out of our lives in extraordinary, unselfconscious, loving, and lavish gratitude to our Savior?

Receiving grace means that we must admit that we are inadequate. There is something very attractive about this. If I can be accepted when I am inadequate, then I can stop trying so hard to preserve the illusion that I have it all together, that I don't make mistakes, that I am perfect. Not only is it impossible to be perfect, but trying to be perfect is so *tiring*.

I do not need to present myself to God as a spotless object. Grace means God cares about me, not my failures, my insecurities, or my reputation. It means God cares more about what is inside than what others see on the outside. God does not see me as an issue or a burden, but as a person. In this way, the Spirit nudges us to give up our quest for our own righteousness and to accept his grace.

CONCLUSION: SEEING GRACE

Jesus asks Simon, "Do you see this woman?" (Luke 7:44).[17] His question does more than point to the woman as an example for a lesson. It is also an invitation for Simon to see her in the same way that he does. It is an invitation for him to change his view from condemnation of

---

17. Thanks go to Julie C. Maxham, whose master's thesis first caused me to stop and consider more seriously the significance of Jesus' remark. "Witness, Discipleship, and Hospitality: A Lukan Theology of Women in the Ministry of Jesus" (ThM thesis, Talbot School of Theology, 2017), 122.

her as someone who has fallen far short of God's law to acceptance of her as one who has received grace and loves in extraordinary ways.[18]

Whom does Simon see when he looks at her? A sinner. Whom does Jesus see? Someone God loves.

I don't want my self-righteousness to blind me to God's grace, in myself and others. Philip Yancey relays a story in his book *What's So Amazing about Grace?* about a friend who was trying to help a prostitute, perhaps someone like the woman in our story. Addicted to drugs, she even rented out her two-year-old daughter to men for sex. However, when he asked her about getting help from a church, he said she responded in this way: "I will never forget the look of pure, naïve shock that crossed her face. 'Church!' she cried. 'Why would I ever go there? I was already feeling terrible about myself. They'd just make me feel worse.'"[19]

Why would this woman run away from the church when the woman in the Gospel story was drawn to Jesus? What is it about the grace that Jesus offers that draws people to him, makes them feel safe, and changes their lives? And what keeps us from demonstrating that grace to others? To ourselves?

I wonder if the woman in the story ever thought that she, a rejected and humiliated sinner, would end up being a role model. She, who probably thought she had nothing to offer, shows me that the more I let go of my need to be perfect, the more I can receive his grace. I think it would be good if we could all be more like her.

---

18. Green, *Gospel of Luke*, 311–12. "This Pharisee represented accepted social conventions in the larger Palestinian world; … Jesus has a different vantage point from which to make sense of this encounter."

19. Philip Yancey, *What's So Amazing about Grace?* (Grand Rapids: Zondervan, 1997), 11.

MAJOR TAKEAWAYS

1. The parable of the two debtors teaches us that great forgiveness leads to great love from the one forgiven.
2. The two characters in the parable relate to Simon and the woman who anoints Jesus as the one who has been forgiven little and the one who had been forgiven much.
3. However, there is irony in Jesus' comment about the relationship between forgiveness and love, for ultimately, there is no one who has been forgiven "little."
4. Therefore, the parable is aimed toward confronting Simon with his inability to see that he needs to be forgiven "much."
5. The extraordinary love the woman shows Jesus comes from her recognition of her own spiritual poverty and the magnitude of what she has received.
6. As a result, the parable challenges us: are we willing to see our own need for forgiveness, or if we will stay in our self-righteousness and resist God's gift?

QUESTIONS

1. What is your initial response to the woman? Why do you think you react to her in this way?
2. Imagine that you are Simon. What would cause you to respond to the woman like he did? Is there anyone you respond to in this way? Why?

3. Continue imagining that you are Simon. What would prevent you from receiving Jesus' forgiveness? What does prevent you from receiving Jesus' forgiveness?

4. Imagine how the woman might have felt. What keeps you from realizing the greatness of God's forgiveness toward you?

5. Why do you think that great forgiveness leads to great love? How have you seen this in your life or someone else's?

GRACE FOR MY NEIGHBOR

THE PARABLE OF THE GOOD
SAMARITAN (LUKE 10:25–37)

On one occasion an expert in the law stood up to test Jesus. "Teacher," he asked, "what must I do to inherit eternal life?"

"What is written in the Law?" he replied. "How do you read it?"

He answered, "'Love the Lord your God with all your heart and with all your soul and with all your strength and with all your mind'; and, 'Love your neighbor as yourself.'"

"You have answered correctly," Jesus replied. "Do this and you will live."

But he wanted to justify himself, so he asked Jesus, "And who is my neighbor?"

In reply Jesus said: "A man was going down from Jerusalem to Jericho, when was attacked by robbers. They stripped him of his clothes, beat him and went away, leaving him half dead. A priest happened to be going down the same road, and when he saw the man,

*he passed by on the other side. So too, a Levite, when he
came to the place and saw him, passed by on the other
side. But a Samaritan, as he traveled, came where the
man was; and when he saw him, he took pity on him.
He went to him and bandaged his wounds, pouring on
oil and wine. Then he put the man on his own donkey,
brought him to an inn and took care of him. The next
day he took out two denarii and gave them to the innkeeper. 'Look after him,' he said, 'and when I return, I
will reimburse you for any extra expense you may have.'*

*"Which of these three do you think was a neighbor
to the man who fell into the hands of robbers?"*

*The expert in the law replied, "The one who had
mercy on him."*

Jesus told him, "Go and do likewise."

INTRODUCTION

"Good Samaritan Helps Family Stranded on Side of Road," "Good
Samaritan Funds Children's Hospital," "Woman Saved from Burning
House by Good Samaritan." How many times have you seen newspa-
per headlines like this? Stories about people who are selfless and sacrificial are wonderful and uplifting. They take us out of our doldrums
and cynicism and remind us that there is still good in the world and
people who will help strangers, even if it costs them dearly.

Here is one recent story that has moved me profoundly. A man
opened fire in a Florida airport while people were waiting for their
luggage. As one woman, Annika Dean, began to understand what was
happening, she also realized in horror that the shooter was coming
toward her. She hid behind a luggage cart and lay down on the floor,
waiting for the gunman to approach. At this point, an elderly man, a
complete stranger to Dean, climbed on top of her and told her he

would protect her. They lay quietly on the floor as gunshots rang over them, but neither one was hit. As she described the ordeal, "He brought me comfort during the most terrifying experience of my life." Of the man himself, she said, "He's just a hero. He just wanted to protect me."

Good Samaritans are heroes. They come to our aid, protect us, and comfort us. They inspire by their example and remind us of the people we want to be. But what if good Samaritans are something more? What if, instead of just giving us an example of what it means to do good, they also show what inside of us is bad, ugly, and in need of God's redemption? What if good Samaritans teach not only by inspiring us to be better people, but also by revealing what keeps us from truly loving God and others?

WHAT DOES IT ACTUALLY MEAN TO BE A SAMARITAN?

Contrary to popular belief, a good Samaritan, or rather, a Samaritan, is not simply someone who helps someone in distress. That is the way we use the term in popular culture, of course, but "Samaritan" has a much deeper biblical meaning, one that was not nearly as pleasant or inspirational. Simply put, Samaritans were seen as traitors to their faith and were hated by the Jews.

The Samaritans were a mixed race, only partly Israelite. Their origins are usually traced back to the exile. Assyria conquered the northern kingdom of Israel, including Samaria, seven hundred years before Jesus' birth, and the king of Assyria settled the area with people from foreign lands.

The Samaritans were seen as having compromised the faith. They worshiped other gods and departed from the law (2 Kgs 17:24–41). They only recognized the first five books of the Old Testament, known as the Pentateuch.[1] They also worshiped at a rival temple built on Mount Gerazim rather than Mount Zion.[2]

A Jewish document from around 200 BC describes the Jews' animosity toward Samaritans, whose religious center was in Shechem:[3]

> Two nations my soul detests,
> And the third is not even a people;
> Those who live in Seir, and the Philistines,
> And the foolish people that live in Shechem. (Sir 50:25–26)

The Jews despised the Samaritans, but it is a Samaritan who helps the man. The point of the story is that it is a Samaritan who does the good deed. The Greek even emphasizes that it is a Samaritan doing this because "Samaritan" occurs first in the sentence.

WHY DID JESUS TELL A PARABLE ABOUT A SAMARITAN?

So why did Jesus make someone who was so hated the hero of the story? We begin by asking why Jesus told the parable in the first place. The entire story begins not with the parable itself, but several verses earlier, in Luke 10:25, when a lawyer comes to Jesus and wants to "test" him. He asks Jesus, "Teacher, what must I do to inherit eternal life?" Jesus tells him to look at the law, and the man replies that the law instructs him to love God "'with all your heart and with all your soul and with all your strength and with all your mind'; and, 'Love your neighbor as yourself'" (Luke 10:27), a statement that combines

---

1. Everett Ferguson, *Backgrounds of Early Christianity*, 2nd ed. (Grand Rapids: Eerdmans, 1993), 500–501.

2. This provides the context for John 4:20, when the Samaritan woman says to Jesus, "Our ancestors worshiped on this mountain, but you Jews claim that the place where we must worship is in Jerusalem."

3. Shechem is a town located on the border of the hill country of Ephraim (Josh 20:7), in the valley between Mount Ebal and Mount Gerazim. "Shechem," in *The Baker Illustrated Bible Dictionary*, ed. Tremper Longman III (Grand Rapids: Baker, 2013), 1514–15.

Deuteronomy 6:5 and Leviticus 19:18. When Jesus instructs him to follow this teaching, the lawyer responds one more time: "And who is my neighbor?" It is in response to this question that Jesus tells the parable of the good Samaritan.

The lawyer's encounter with Jesus reveals something about his heart. He asks Jesus who is his neighbor because he wants "to justify himself" (Luke 10:29). This may mean he wants to justify his earlier question, since Jesus turned it around to challenge him and prompt him to give his own answer.[4] However, it is more likely that he wants to be confident in his position of seeking to minimize the obedience required rather than accept the total obedience that Jesus demands.[5]

The lawyer's question, "Who is my neighbor?" implies that he thinks there is such a thing as a nonneighbor—in other words, someone to whom he does not need to extend mercy and compassion. Traditionally, "neighbor" would refer to a fellow Jew, so his viewpoint is not that unusual.[6]

The Jews understood their relationships and responsibilities according to a series of concentric circles. If the Jew were at the center, the expanding circles would include first immediate relatives, then kinsmen, and then all other Jews. Foundational to the circles was determining who was worthy of aid based on self-interest and ethnic belonging. Lines were drawn so that those inside received help while those outside did not.[7] The Jews saw their "neighbors" as their fellow Jews, and excluded foreigners and Samaritans.

---

4. I. Howard Marshall, *The Gospel of Luke*, New International Greek Testament Commentary (Grand Rapids: Eerdmans, 1978), 447.

5. Darrell L. Bock, *Luke 9:51–24:53, Baker Exegetical Commentary on the New Testament* (Grand Rapids: Baker, 1996), 1028.

6. Arland J. Hultgren, *The Parables of Jesus* (Grand Rapids: Eerdmans, 2000), 94.

7. Simon J. Kistemaker, *The Parables: Understanding the Stories Jesus Told* (Grand Rapids: Baker, 1980), 141.

A first-century Jew would have understood and accepted the lawyer's question. Jesus, however, does not accept that limited understanding. He instead applies the golden rule and challenges the lawyer to reconsider who is his neighbor.[8] Jesus' response indicates that his teaching is about caring for all who are created in God's image, rather than classifying people and finding different obligations for each category of persons. As a result, Jesus will teach the man about the deeper meaning of the law and what is lacking in his heart.

THE PARABLE

Jesus tells the lawyer a parable about a man going from Jerusalem to Jericho who is attacked by robbers. The roads in Israel at that time were rough, and travel was slow. In addition, the Jericho road was particularly known for being treacherous. Although the road was well traveled, it was an inviting place for bandits since it descended sharply through barren and rocky limestone hills. On this road, people commonly traveled in groups for fear of robbers.[9]

It is here that the man is brutally beaten and left half-dead, a scene that would not have been surprising to Jesus' hearers, who would have been familiar with the hazards of traveling that road. The question is, then, Who will help him? Jesus describes the responses of three people who encounter the desperate man, all of whom have a specific significance to the lawyer.

The term "lawyer," or *nomikos* in the Greek, refers to one who is an expert in the law. This person is sometimes called a "scribe" (*grammateus*) in other passages, or one who is trained to teach and interpret the law.[10] Since his life revolves around the Jewish law, it would be a shock to hear that the first two people who pass by without helping

---

8. Kistemaker, *Parables*, 141–42.

9. David Wenham, *The Parables of Jesus* (Downers Grove, IL: InterVarsity, 1989), 155.

10. Hultgren, *Parables of Jesus*, 95.

the injured man were a priest and a Levite, who were considered to be the Jews' highest religious officials. The priests were in charge of the temple and were seen as the prime representatives of the Jewish religion. The Levites were second-ranking figures in the life of the temple. Their duties included music and security as singers and gatekeepers (1 Chr 9:14–44; Ezra 2:40–42).[11] They also helped the priests with the services (Num 3–4, 1 Chr 23). The lawyer would have expected the exemplary Jewish leaders to help the man and would have been shocked, even offended, that they did not stop.

In contrast to the priest's and Levite's refusal to help the man, the Samaritan bandages his wounds and takes him to an inn. Furthermore, he pays for him out of his own pocket. He gives the innkeeper two silver coins, or in some translations, two denarii, which would be two days' wages. To the amazement of the lawyer, the Samaritan, the one who is despised and seen as not honoring God's law, is the one who helps. The ones considered the epitome of law keeping do not. Jesus' parable turns the lawyer's world upside down. Can he admit that the Samaritan is the one who is "good"?

Therefore, the parable is much more than a story about doing good to strangers. The most powerful point is to expose the lawyer's self-righteousness and prejudice. He does not want to acknowledge that the hated Samaritan is the one who selflessly helps. Notice that in the end when Jesus asks who was the neighbor to the man, the lawyer cannot even bring himself to say "the Samaritan," but only "the one who had mercy on him." The lawyer knows the "right" things to do, but has an inadequate knowledge of how to show love. He is unable to love the Samaritan.

---

11. Ferguson, *Early Christianity*, 531.

LESSONS OF TRANSFORMATION
FROM THE GOOD SAMARITAN

The parable challenges us to act compassionately, as the Samaritan does (Luke 10:33). He shows that love focuses on the person in need, while the lawyer wants to know what the law expects of him. The lawyer does not understand the greater spirit behind the law. He hopes he can *do* something to gain eternal life, but does not understand the heart of God.

The passage shows how much we can miss when we make following the law the foundation of our faith. The lawyer, the priest, and the Levite all miss the point. They are religious, but not faithful. If the lawyer truly loved God, as he states so boldly in his first answer to Jesus, this love would be manifested in his compassion and love toward others. However, he thinks in terms of rules and requirements, rather than grace and love. That the lawyer asked the question "Who is my neighbor?" at the beginning shows that he is focused on fulfilling requirements, or checklists of outward religious actions, rather than being transformed internally so he can make himself available to love others.

The Samaritan not only comes to the aid of the wounded man, but he also provides extravagant care. He cares for his wounds, bandaging them and "pouring on oil and wine," which would be the same as ointment and disinfectant today. Luke tells us that he puts him on his own donkey, which he had likely been riding on himself, and "took care of him." He pays the innkeeper two silver coins and offers to reimburse him for any additional expenses. This is quite a generous offer considering it is possible that the two denarii themselves would have paid for twenty-four nights at the inn![12]

---

12. Wenham, *Parables of Jesus*, 157.

The parable calls us to become people of compassion, but to do this we must also confront our own prejudices. Just as the lawyer would have been offended at seeing the Samaritan, we can see where our own prejudices are. Who do we think are the "good" people? Who are the "bad" people? While we profess to love everyone, it probably will not take much soul-searching to see the deep resentments and stereotypes that we hold.

It can be helpful to try to place yourself in the parable. Think about the person you admire—the pastor who preaches expertly from the Scriptures, the elder who faithfully shows up every Sunday to teach your favorite Sunday school class and greet people, your wise aunt who always knows the right thing to say. What if you saw that person acting in a less than compassionate way to someone who really needs it?

Even more so, who is someone you would least expect to show compassion? An atheist? A terrorist? A sexual predator? But we don't even need to be that extreme to reveal hearts, because it is not difficult to find where we consider ourselves superior to other people. For example, if you are a hard and faithful worker, how do you feel about the person who seems to get ahead because he talks a good game and has everyone fooled? Or, if you pride yourself in your faithful service to your church, what if the hero is the person who comes to church every Sunday, never gets involved, and only seems to want to be there for the social benefit? It is hard to admit that the person who really annoys you (and here is where you see how annoyed you really are) is the one whose example you should applaud and emulate.

Here is the place where we can pause and ask the Lord to show us who is the Samaritan in our lives and why. If your response is conviction in your heart toward this person and newfound humility, then the parable has done its work. It is important to notice your initial response. If it is not the "right one," or the one this parable encourages us toward, consider asking for God's help in changing your reaction so that you may experience the conviction and humility that this parable points to.

The parable not only teaches us that we should show compassion to everyone, but also that our hardened hearts prevent us from loving others as we should, that we too make distinctions and draw limits, and that we do so because we harbor deep prejudices against others. We like to judge without taking the log out of our eyes (Matt 7:5) because it makes us feel good about ourselves. As in the parable of the Pharisee and the tax collector (Luke 18:9–14), we thank God that we are not like the "other people" who have fallen away because we are satisfied with our own virtue and feel better in comparison with those who are not as virtuous as we are.

But our self-righteousness blinds us and leaves us unable to respond to grace. The lawyer demonstrates a desire to live by the law, to discharge his duty by fulfilling requirements. It is only when we admit to the dark places in our own hearts that we have the space to allow God to transform them by his grace. As Jeremiah 17:9 observes, "The heart is deceitful above all things and beyond cure." We need to ask ourselves the difficult question of how we try to "justify" ourselves to find the clues to how we harden our hearts and keep them closed to God. But in being willing to ask this, we make ourselves available for God's ever-present grace.

The parable can confront us in many ways. While the lawyer would have been understandably shocked to see the priest and the Levite pass by the wounded man, we can also ask, Why did they pass him by? Although Scripture does not tell us explicitly, there are some possibilities. Perhaps they were concerned that if the man were dead, touching him would have made them ceremonially unclean, as described in Leviticus 21:1 and Ezekiel 44:25.[13] The description of the man as

---

13. Ezekiel 44:25 says, "A priest must not defile himself by going near a dead person." In the same way, Lev 21:1 says, "A priest must not make himself ceremonially

"half dead" (Luke 10:30) may indicate that the priest could not be sure whether he was dead or alive unless he touched him. The only way to maintain ceremonial purity was by leaving the man alone.[14] If the priest were headed to Jerusalem, he would not have wanted to become unclean. If he were coming from Jerusalem, it would be inconvenient to have to go back again.[15]

Perhaps he did not want to take the chance in helping a stranger. There was a Jewish tradition in which one should not help anyone thought to be a "sinner."[16] While someone might benefit from helping someone who was devout, people feared that the dishonest person would take advantage of the person's kindness and cause harm.[17] Maybe the priest did not want to get involved and was afraid for his own safety. The Levite may have mirrored the priest's caution. Although we cannot know for sure, the inclusion of two religious leaders in a parable told to the lawyer indicates that Jesus wants to show the limitations of life by the law.

---

unclean for any of his people who die."

14. Leon Morris, *Luke*, Tyndale New Testament Commentaries (Leicester, UK: Inter-Varsity Press; Grand Rapids: Eerdmans, 1988), 207.

15. Stephen Wright, *Tales Jesus Told: An Introduction to the Narrative Parables of Jesus* (Carlisle, UK: Paternoster, 2002), 37–38.

16. A sinner can be defined as "a person who is guilty of violating the will of God as revealed in the law and thus under the danger of God's wrath." Dwayne H. Adams, *The Sinner in Luke*, Evangelical Theological Society Monograph Series (Eugene, OR: Pickwick, 2008), 195.

17. "Do good to the devout, and you will be repaid—if not by them, certainly by the Most High. No good comes to one who persists in evil and to one who does not give alms. Give to the devout, but do not help the sinner. Do good to the humble, but do not give to the ungodly; hold back their bread, and do not give it to them, for by means of it they might subdue you; then you will receive twice as much evil for all the good you have done to them. ... Give to the one who is good, but do not help the sinner" (Sirach 12:1–7); John G. Snaith, *Ecclesiasticus* (Cambridge: Cambridge University Press, 1974), 64. The sentiment provides a stark contrast with Jesus' words in the Sermon on the Mount, where he urges loving one's enemies (Matt 5:44).

The Samaritan follows a different way. Instead of following religious regulations or being concerned for his own well-being, he "took pity" on the injured man (Luke 10:33). The Samaritan, not the lawyer, is the one who truly fulfills Jesus' command to love his neighbor as himself (10:27). He has internalized what the law truly represents, including God's compassion.

RESPONDING TO THE PARABLE

One of the questions that then challenges us personally is, Whom do I pass by, and why? I would guess that one of the biggest obstacles to compassion is that we are occupied with other things. On the one hand, we are busy. We are occupied with so many other things, often good things. We don't mean to pass people by. It's just that we don't see them because our minds are preoccupied.

But perhaps we don't act in the way we want to not only because we are merely preoccupied, but also because we are self-preoccupied. We don't see the real needs of others because we spend too much time seeing our own.

I went through a period several years ago where I became particularly aware of my selfishness, desire to protect myself, and general hardness toward others. However, I rationalized it was because I was tired and overworked. I had a sabbatical coming up (one of those great perks of being a professor!) and was eagerly looking forward to it. Not only would it be a welcome break, but I also thought that without the daily pressures of deadlines, meetings, grading, and students, I would be a much nicer person. After all, my selfishness was just due to feeling a bit burned out and not having enough time to be generous with people.

It turned out I was very wrong. The sabbatical didn't make me a nicer person. In fact, I found that in a lot of ways I became an even more selfish person now that I wasn't required to fulfill my duties to others and instead had control over my time. This was "my time," and I became resentful of anyone who intruded on it.

I realized that all of my excuses were just that: excuses. The sabbatical allowed what was deep in my heart to become evident, and it could not be covered up by religious requirements. I was the most important person in my life, and it showed.

How do we move past our own selfishness, prejudices, and fears to be moved by compassion, by seeing the needs of another made in the image of God? Let's consider the lawyer's initial answer to Christ—"'Love the Lord your God with all your heart and with all your soul and with all your strength and with all your mind'; and 'Love your neighbor as yourself'" (Luke 10:27).

As mentioned earlier, for the Jew the term "neighbor" was understood as something that could be defined according to predefined boundaries. At the heart of the lawyer's question is the assumption that not everyone is his "neighbor," and so he attempts to define boundaries for his obligation to love.

While this way of thinking was not unusual in the Judaism of the day, for Jesus, this is no excuse to miss the point of the law and the goal for our hearts. The lawyer and Jesus represent two different perspectives, which reveal much about how we approach others. The lawyer's approach is to control and define. There is a sense of security in the way he thinks, knowing who is in and out. We know what our duties and responsibilities are. We know who is for us and who is against us. We have a sense of belonging and identity. But this way of thinking also distances us from those who are outside the circle, giving us a reason not to care. The second and greater perspective is open to whatever need arises and so is able to see the need. It is more uncontrolled, unpredictable, and therefore scary. Who knows what we will be called to do? What if we do not like the person who needs our help? What if we actually despise them? This is the way that calls us to be willing to die to self in order to respond to the needs of the world. It is the way of Christ, and it is hard.

The challenge of the parable is in the response. While we may criticize the lawyer for being so rigid, for actually trying to define who and who is not his neighbor, he is also very much like you and me. I know that every day I make decisions in terms of whom I want to help and whom I will ignore. The challenge is to be able respond like the lawyer should have responded, allowing the parable to penetrate our hearts and expose where we shut people out, leave them behind, or allow our critical thoughts to lead to judgment and uncaring.

The object of compassion and sympathy is not just the man on the side of the road, but also the Samaritan. The parable calls us to ask ourselves, Who is the Samaritan in my life? Who is the person whom I don't want to admit could do something good so I can continue to hate/despise/resent them? And perhaps most importantly, Why? What does this reveal about my own heart? Asking these questions can become the gateway to revealing the motivations beneath our hidden animosities as we ponder why we hold them and what they provide for us. How we respond can tell us much about our heart.

CONCLUSION: GRACE FOR OTHERS

It is relatively easy to fulfill one's duty. It is much harder to be motivated by love. The parable confronts us with the true depths and reality of our love and willingness to follow Jesus' way of unconditional love by causing us to think about how we would respond to others. As one New Testament scholar states it, *"one's enemy is the most important neighbor of all."*[18] By examining our response to those who have the least to give us, or who might actually harm us, we discover the true state of our heart.

---

18. Craig L. Blomberg, *Preaching the Parables: From Responsible Interpretation to Powerful Proclamation* (Grand Rapids: Baker, 2004), 64, italics original.

So what happens when our heart is lacking? It is good to remember that while our first response may be guilt and shame, the apostle Paul reassures us that God's love for us is boundless and transcends our very human frailties. In Romans 5:10, he boldly states, "For if, while we were God's enemies, we were reconciled to him through the death of his Son, how much more, having been reconciled, shall we be saved through his life!" God loved us when we were least lovable and continues to do so. Paul says we can rest in this fact of God's unchanging acceptance of us.

The Samaritan's generosity reflects God's abundant grace. God does not mete grace to us grudgingly, but gives to us lavishly and extravagantly. Romans 5:5 tell us that God has "poured out" his love into our hearts through the Spirit. His grace is abundant, extravagant, overwhelming.

And in knowing God's love, we are also changed in our capacity to love. John 15:12 tells us, "Love each other as I have loved you." We respond to God's love by loving others. The love of God and the love of his children are in many ways inseparable. We might even say that to love God is to love your neighbor.[19]

In this way, the lawyer's response may reveal a key to our hearts: "Love the Lord your God with all your heart and with all your soul and with all your strength and with all your mind" (Luke 10:27, which comes from Deut 6:5). The verse describes a love that involves the whole person. It speaks of a total devotion to God that ultimately leads to both love of God and love of humanity.

As we saw in the previous lessons on the woman who anoints Jesus and the prodigal son, God's bountiful and abundant love can cause us to respond in a similar way. This may be the ultimate lesson

---

19. "Judaism also recognized that if humans were created in God's image to love God, one must love humans." Darrell L. Bock, *Luke 9:51–24:53*, Baker Exegetical Commentary on the New Testament (Grand Rapids: Baker, 1996), 1025.

of the parable. To live by our own works is to be limited in our ability to love, just as the lawyer was. Ultimately, we cannot love others as we should. But God has given us someone who can help us—his own Spirit. We can only give God's love to others as we participate in the lavish grace of the kingdom.

MAJOR TAKEAWAYS

1. A good Samaritan is more than a person who does something to help someone else. Good Samaritans have experienced heart transformation, and their outward actions are compelled by the love of God.

2. The lawyer tries to gain eternal life by following the law, but his focus on external actions and duty causes him to miss the true meaning of the law.

3. The lawyer is shocked that the most respected religious figures pass by the man without helping him.

4. The lawyer reveals his prejudices when he is offended that the hated Samaritan is the one who helps the man.

5. Through the parable, Jesus teaches that heart change comes from the transformative love of God, so that we can truly love God and others.

6. The parable challenges us to consider the ways in which we harbor prejudices and resentments toward others, and how God can transform our hearts.

QUESTIONS

1. How does knowing the historical background of the lawyer affect the way that you understand him and the questions he asks?

2. The lawyer tries to limit whom he can consider as his "neighbor." In what ways do you tend to narrow your own definition of "neighbor"?

3. How does knowing the historical background of the priest and Levite influence the way you think about their actions? In what ways do you avoid being compassionate and why?

4. What does the good Samaritan risk in stopping to help? What might have outweighed any fear?

5. Without judging their merit, what are some of the rules that you have for yourself in your faith? Ask the Spirit which ones may be beneficial and which might be hindering your spiritual growth. Although the law is good (Rom 7:12; 1 Tim 1:8), the lawyer has reduced his faith to a set of rules that choke the life out of his faith. Prayerfully consider how the Holy Spirit might help you reorchestrate these habits so they flow from a love of God.

6. The power of the parable comes from understanding the cultural significance of priests, Levites, and Samaritans. Reimagine the parable of the good Samaritan in the present day. How would you rewrite the story using modern-day characters?

7. Whom might you expect to be exemplary? Whom would you be shocked to see as the hero? What does your reaction reveal about your own prejudices?

8. Take some extra time to consider who is the Samaritan in your life. In other words, whom do you have trouble accepting as your "neighbor"? Consider how you feel toward that person and why. Note that this could be an individual or a group of people. How can the parable of the good Samaritan help you in your relationship with this person? What concrete steps can you take in this relationship?

FORGIVING GRACE

Then Peter came to Jesus and asked, "Lord, how many times shall I forgive my brother or sister who sins against me? Up to seven times?"

Jesus answered, "I tell you, not seven times, but seventy-seven times.

"Therefore, the kingdom of heaven is like a king who wanted to settle accounts with his servants. As he began the settlement, a man who owed him ten thousand bags of gold [talents] was brought to him. Since he was not able to pay, the master ordered that he and his wife and his children and all that he had be sold to repay the debt.

"At this the servant fell on his knees before him. 'Be patient with me,' he begged, 'and I will pay back everything.' The servant's master took pity on him, canceled the debt and let him go.

"But when that servant went out, he found one of his fellow servants who owed him a hundred silver coins *[denarii]. He grabbed him and began to choke him. 'Pay back what you owe me!' he demanded.*

"His fellow servant fell to his knees and begged him, 'Be patient with me, and I will pay it back.'

"But he refused. Instead, he went off and had the man thrown into prison until he could pay the debt. When the other servants saw what had happened, they were outraged and went and told their master everything that had happened.

"Then the master called the servant in. 'You wicked servant,' he said, 'I canceled all that debt of yours because you begged me to. Shouldn't you have had mercy on your fellow servant just as I had on you?' In anger his master handed him over to the jailers to be tortured, until he should pay back all he owed.

"This is how my heavenly Father will treat each of you unless you forgive your brother or sister from your heart."

INTRODUCTION

On July 17, 2015, twenty-one-year old Dylann Roof entered Emmanuel African Methodist Episcopal Church in Charleston, South Carolina, and was welcomed into a Wednesday night Bible study. An hour later, as the members closed their eyes to pray, he stood up and started shooting. By the time it was over, nine people were dead, with each of the victims having been shot at least five times.[1] In his journal, Roof

---

1. "Autopsies: Each Church Shooting Victim Was Hit at Least 5 Times," *Chicago Tribune*, December 14, 2016, http://www.chicagotribune.com/news/nationworld/ct-charleston-church-shooting-autopsies-20161214-story.html.

stated that he specifically wanted to kill the people in the church because they were black.[2]

It was a horrific act that shattered families and outraged a nation. But perhaps what shocked people even more was the reaction of some of the victims' families. Yes, they wanted justice, but personally, they forgave him. Instead of seeking revenge, they prayed for his soul, despite their own incredible pain.

Nadine Collier, whose mother was one of the victims, told Roof, "I forgive you. You took something very precious away from me. I will never get to talk to her ever again. I will never be able to hold her again, but I forgive you. And have mercy on your soul."[3] Collier's brave words prompted astonishment and questions. How could someone forgive someone like him? In the parable of the unforgiving servant, we learn how central forgiveness is to the Christian life, because forgiveness is at the root of what God shows us in his grace.

THE PARABLE

The parable of the unforgiving servant is introduced by Jesus' exchange with Peter in which the apostle asks him how often he must forgive someone who sins against him. Peter asks whether he should forgive this person up to seven times. Seven is a number that represented fullness, and his proposal is a marked increase to the rabbinic view that three times was enough.[4]

---

2. He also said he originally thought about killing drug dealers but decided against it because he thought they would shoot back. "Dylann Roof's Confession, Journal Details Racist Motivation for Killings," *Chicago Tribune*, December 10, 2016, http://www.chicagotribune.com/news/nationworld/ct-dylann-roof-charleston-shooting-20161209-story.html.

3. Mark Berman, "'I Forgive You': Relatives of Charleston Church Shooting Victims Address Dylann Roof," *Washington Post*, July 19, 2015, https://www.washingtonpost.com/news/post-nation/wp/2015/06/19/i-forgive-you-relatives-of-charleston-church-victims-address-dylann-roof/?utm_term=.52540db7d58e.

4. Donald A. Hagner, *Matthew 14–28*, Word Biblical Commentary 33B (Dallas:

Jesus answers, however, that one should forgive seventy-seven times. The number ten would also symbolize completeness, and so Jesus' number multiplies completeness by completeness and adds yet another completeness. The resulting number would therefore convey the idea of infinity. Jesus is essentially saying that God's mercy is too great to be measured.[5] The parable illustrates how great God's own mercy is toward us. Although seven would be an astounding number for Peter to consider forgiving someone, God's forgiveness toward him is overwhelmingly greater, far beyond Peter's attempt to numerically quantify forgiveness.

Jesus then tells a parable to illustrate his point. A king comes to settle accounts with his servants. The scene is tense. Such an accounting would be like an intensive audit by the Internal Revenue Service, and the tension increases when he finds one servant enormously in debt, owing ten thousand talents.[6] The talent was the highest unit of currency in the ancient Greco-Roman world. It was the equivalent of six thousand denarii. Since a denarius was considered one day's wage for a day laborer, this meant that if the person worked three hundred days out of the year, it would take twenty years to earn one talent. If the servant owed ten thousand talents, the total would come to two hundred thousand years' wages![7] It could appropriately be translated as "billions of dollars."[8] In other words, it was an absurd amount.

Word, 1995), 537.

5. Simon J. Kistemaker, *The Parables: Understanding the Stories Jesus Told* (Grand Rapids: Baker, 1980), 66.

6. Brad H. Young, *The Parables: Jewish Tradition and Christian Interpretation* (Grand Rapids: Baker, 1998), 125.

7. As calculated by Arland J. Hultgren, *The Parables of Jesus* (Grand Rapids: Eerdmans, 2000), 23–24. Another way of considering how large a sum it represented is to note that the annual tax revenue from Herod the Great's kingdom was about nine hundred talents (Josephus, *Jewish Antiquities* 17.11.4).

8. Craig L. Blomberg, *Preaching the Parables: From Responsible Interpretation to Powerful Proclamation* (Grand Rapids: Baker, 2004), 71.

Since the servant cannot pay, the king, now referred to as "master," announces that he and his entire family and all he owns will be sold to pay for the debt, even though it will not come close to covering what he owed. The servant begs for mercy, promising to pay back everything, but it would be impossible for him to repay that much. Not only is the amount hopelessly large, but it would have been extremely difficult for anyone in a Roman prison to earn money at all.[9] But on hearing his plea, the king takes pity on him and cancels the debt.

The servant, freed from his debt and the possibility of enslavement, now goes out and encounters a fellow servant who owes him money. The second servant's debt is much smaller, only one hundred denarii, or about three months' wages. The first servant violently demands repayment, grabbing and choking him. The indebted servant also begs for mercy, using almost exactly the same plea as the first servant did with the king.[10]

But instead of showing mercy like he had received, the first servant throws his fellow servant into prison until he can pay back his debt. We can presume that he would be well aware of how difficult it would be for him to earn enough to pay him back while in prison. His actions are especially startling considering the enormous amount he has just been forgiven. The other servants become greatly distressed, and they report what has happened to the master. This time the king is very angry. Because the servant did not have mercy on his fellow servant as the king had on him, he turns him over to the jailers to be tortured until he can pay back his own debt.

---

9. Blomberg, *Preaching the Parables*, 73.

10. The only difference is that the first servant says he will pay back "everything" (Matt 18:26).

ANSWERING SOME QUESTIONS
ABOUT THE PARABLE

There are a number of questions and concerns that come from the parable. One question is how the king's behavior is related to God. In the beginning of the parable the master is exceedingly generous and gracious. By the end of the parable we are a bit afraid of him. Yes, the servant was ungrateful and unmerciful, but did the master really need to punish him that severely? He not only renews the servant's debt, but also hands him over to the torturers![11]

It would be natural to associate God with the king since in the Old Testament God is king over Israel (e.g., Isa 43:15) and the whole earth (Ps 29:10).[12] The New Testament also emphasizes the theme of the kingdom of God (e.g., Luke 4:43). Some object to seeing God in this way. Although God is the perfect king, human kings are often seen in a negative light in Scripture. After all, Israel's demand for a human king was seen as a rejection of God as their king. It was not that there was necessarily a problem with the institution of kingship, but rather the people's motives in seeking a king were wrong as they wanted one so they could be like the other nations (1 Sam 8:5, 19–20). In particular, it seems they wanted a king who would be a military ruler to build an army and protect them from their enemies (1 Sam 8:20).[13] The prophet Samuel warns them that having a king like they are seeking will lead to their oppression under his rule. As one author

---

11. Hultgren notes that Jewish law allowed for flogging, which would be considered close to torture, although only as discipline, not as retaliation (*Parables of Jesus*, 28). However, Hagner observes that torture was common in Roman prisons (*Matthew 14–28*, 540). Wenham notes that it was used by people such as Herod to collect debts. See David Wenham, *The Parables of Jesus* (Downers Grove, IL: InterVarsity, 1989), 153.

12. Another reason the disciples would have easily associated the king with God is that the rabbinic literature also uses kings to stand for God (Blomberg, *Preaching the Parables*, 73).

13. Ronald F. Youngblood, "1, 2 Samuel," in *Expositor's Bible Commentary*, ed. Frank E. Gaebelein (Grand Rapids: Zondervan, 1992), 613.

describes, "the average Israelite would soon be little more than chattel at the disposal of his monarch."[14] Overall, the image of a king brought up images of wealth, power, and ruthlessness, and so these would be the expectations when used in a story.[15]

Since Jesus associates the king with God in his generosity toward the servant, it is likely that this identification is meant to be carried through the rest of the parable. This specific parable even begins by saying that the point of the parable is to describe what the kingdom is "like" (Matt 18:23).

The key may be in the way the king calls the servant "wicked" after he refuses to grant mercy to his fellow servant. By his actions, the servant has revealed his true nature. While he was expected to receive the king's grace in a way that would cause him to show mercy to others, he only takes advantage of him. He is willing to accept personal benefit from his master, but will not let it penetrate his heart and transform him. Therefore, it is not that the master is harsh as much as the servant is wicked.[16]

A second question arises from the observation that the first servant loses the forgiveness of his debt. This causes some to ask whether it implies that one can lose one's salvation. That is a difficult question, but it may be instructive to see that only one chapter later, Jesus explains that not everyone who says they are a follower is truly a follower. "Not everyone who says to me, 'Lord, Lord,' will enter the kingdom of heaven, but only the one who does the will of my Father who is in heaven. Many will say to me on that day, 'Lord, Lord, did we not

---

14. Samuel's view of human kingship here might come from his observations of the institution in Canaanite society (Youngblood, "1, 2 Samuel," 614).

15. Hultgren, *Parables of Jesus*, 25.

16. Wilkins explains that the comment about the servant being "tortured" is a reference to what happened to people in debtors' prisons, which would also be "a harsh metaphorical allusion to an eternal destiny of judgment." See Michael J. Wilkins, *Matthew*, NIV Application Commentary (Grand Rapids: Zondervan, 2004), 624.

prophesy in your name and in your name drive out demons and in your name perform many miracles?' Then I will tell them plainly, 'I never knew you. Away from me, you evildoers!'" (Matt 7:21–23). He does not say that he no longer knows them, but that he never knew them.[17] Ultimately, though, since the point of the parable is to teach about our need to forgive others, it is probably best not to try to come to theological conclusions on issues that the parable is not intended to address. Although comparisons can be made between the characters in the parable and their real-life counterparts, this does not mean that every detail in a parable has theological significance and a direct divine or human reference.

A third question is whether human forgiveness is a prerequisite to divine forgiveness. This was taught in some Jewish documents. For example, one explains,

> The vengeful will face the Lord's vengeance,
> for he keeps a strict account of their sins.
> Forgive your neighbor the wrong he has done,
> and then your sins will be pardoned when you
> pray.
> Does anyone harbor anger against another,
> and expect healing from the Lord?
> If one has no mercy toward another like himself,
> can he then seek pardon for his own sins?
> (Sirach 28:1–3)

---

17. We find similar statements elsewhere in the New Testament, such as 1 John 2:19, "They went out from us, but they did not really belong to us. For if they had belonged to us, they would have remained with us; but their going showed that none of them belonged to us."

Although the author thinks that one must forgive in order to receive God's forgiveness, this would go against the teaching in Scripture. Because we are imperfect, we would never be able to be forgiven. It is sometimes thought that the Lord's Prayer teaches human forgiveness as a condition for divine forgiveness (Matt 6:12; Luke 11:4). However, it is better to see the statement about forgiving others as related to the request for divine forgiveness as following the logic of moving from the lesser to the greater. If we can forgive in all our fallenness, surely we can trust a merciful God to forgive us.[18]

Rather than human forgiveness being necessary for God's forgiveness, the parable teaches the opposite. We can forgive because we have first been forgiven (Eph 4:32). Divine forgiveness is the means for human forgiveness. We are able to forgive because we have been forgiven much. The focus is on the greatness of God's actions toward us.

WHY FORGIVENESS?

Whatever forgiveness we might extend is nothing compared to what God has done for us. It was common for people to be sold into slavery as payment for debts. This was a situation that the ancient audience would be familiar with. We see this practice elsewhere in the Gospels and the Old Testament.[19] Sometimes people even sold

---

18. Leon Morris, *Luke*, Tyndale New Testament Commentaries (Leicester, UK: Inter-Varsity Press; Grand Rapids: Eerdmans, 1988), 212.

19. Such as Matt 5:25–26 (also Luke 12:58–59), "Settle matters quickly with your adversary who is taking you to court. Do it while you are still together on the way, or your adversary may hand you over to the judge, and the judge may hand you over to the officer, and you may be thrown into prison. Truly I tell you, you will not get out until you have paid the last penny." Exodus 22:3 records, "Anyone who steals must certainly make restitution, but if they have nothing, they must be sold to pay for their theft." Second Kings 4:1 refers to a creditor coming to take two young sons of a widow as slaves to pay for the debt of the deceased husband. Nehemiah 5:5 also speaks of the enslavement of children to pay off debts. Young notes that this practice is also recorded in the Greek papyri and the rabbinic literature (*Parables*, 126).

themselves into slavery voluntarily so they would be cared for.[20]

But while the threat of prison for debt was real, the amount the first servant owed—ten thousand talents—is startling. Some have wondered how he could have accumulated such a large debt. Possibly he was a governor who collected taxes for the king and misused the funds. However he accumulated it, though, the main point is the hyperbole shows how staggering and impossible his debt was and so how great the forgiveness.[21]

God's amazing generosity toward us compels us to be generous to others. As one writer explains, "Since you have been forgiven so much, how can you not forgive the other person?"[22] The proper response to such grace is to give grace to others. We treat people not just as we would like to be treated but how we have been treated by God, and even then, whatever we can do is only a small shadow compared with what God has done for us.

Truly receiving God's forgiveness can change the way we look at other people and their offenses against us. God's mercy is not simply something that is received once, but rather is "a persistent power that pervades all of life."[23] One of the ways we see this power is the way God's mercy on our behalf can open the way to relationship with our fellow fallen humans. Can we accept forgiveness in a way that transforms the way we view others, who are also created in the divine image? We may not be able to pay God back for all the wrong we have done, but we can extend the forgiveness we have received to others.[24]

---

20. Blomberg, *Preaching the Parables*, 72. In these and other ways, we can see important differences between slavery in biblical times and slavery in American history.

21. Wilkins, *Matthew*, 623.

22. Hultgren, *Parables of Jesus*, 29.

23. Herman Ridderbos, *Matthew* (Grand Rapids: Zondervan, 1987), 346.

24. As France puts it, for the servant to forgive his fellow servant was "an act of generosity which was within his power." R. T. France, *Matthew*, New International Commentary on the New Testament (Grand Rapids: Eerdmans, 2007), 708.

A key to understanding forgiveness is compassion. The king canceled the first servant's debt because he felt "compassion" (Matt 18:27 NASB) for him. Do you believe that God forgives you out of compassion, because he cares deeply for you? It is the king's compassion that led him to forgive the servant, but the servant failed to be moved in the same way, and so was unable to do the same to his fellow servant.

FORGIVENESS IN THE COMMUNITY

The parable occurs within a larger context of teachings about relationships in community. Right before the passage is Jesus' lesson on how the community should handle situations when a church member sins against another member. The person who has been sinned against should go directly to the other person and "point out their fault" (Matt 18:15). The hope is that he will listen and repent. However, if this does not happen, the offended person is to take along two or three witnesses, and if this then does not work, the matter should be brought before the entire church.[25] It is important to note that the goal of the process is to restore the person who sinned both in his or her own spiritual life and in the life of the entire community. The final objective is reconciliation, rather than punishment, and bringing the person back to faithfulness.[26]

If the person refuses to repent even at the urging of the entire congregation, Jesus says to "treat them as you would a pagan or a tax collector" (Matt 18:17). This does not mean they are entirely rejected and banned from the congregation. On the contrary, the church is still to exhibit compassion to encourage them to repent. However, they are

---

25. Of course, care and discretion must be used in involving the entire church. Wilkins notes that this process seems most effective by bringing church leaders into the process rather than something like making an announcement from the pulpit (*Matthew*, 619).

26. Wilkins, *Matthew*, 618.

not incorporated into the intimate life of the body of believers.[27] The ultimate goal is the restoration of the fellowship of the community.

Forgiveness is to be a hallmark of the Christian community, which is understood as a family. Paul recognizes that the believers will continue to battle sin and will therefore hurt and wound one another. Therefore, it is important for them to remember to "bear with each other and forgive one another if any of you has a grievance against someone." But in this Christ is their model and source, as they are to forgive as the Lord forgave you (Col 3:13; also Eph 4:32).

All too often it seems that the world is moving increasingly toward insults, retribution, and hostility. We see it on the news, in our communities, on the freeways. A few years ago my stepdaughter was putting money in a parking meter when a car sideswiped another car and sent that car careening into hers. We were thankful that it didn't happen thirty seconds earlier when she was getting out of her car. The first car took off and left the elderly woman in the second car to take the blame for the accident. I have heard of so many hit-and-run accidents that when I hear about someone who actually stays at the scene of an accident that they caused, I am surprised, and then saddened at my surprise.

What would our churches look like if we sought reconciliation with one another, if we were able to forgive one another? It's hard to imagine the world not noticing it.

RESPONDING TO THE PARABLE

So how can we forgive? We see in the parable itself that the fellow servants are "greatly distressed" (NIV 1984) when they see what the first servant does (Matt 18:31). The word for "distressed" can also be translated as "outraged" (NIV 2011). They are so upset they report the

---

27. Wilkins, *Matthew,* 619.

servant to the king, and we are meant to relate to their anger.[28] We are to see how ludicrous it is not to forgive other people when we have been forgiven so much. We are to follow the example of the king.

Forgiveness allows us to trust God. To forgive is to let go of the wrong, of the desire for revenge, and in the end, a release of the situation to the Lord.[29] On the other side, a lack of forgiveness can cause great damage to our souls. An unforgiving spirit can be "a refusal to let go a wrong suffered that locks an individual into a prison of his own making, where resentment, bitterness, and anger become one's constant companion."[30] Unfortunately, the path we too often pursue is not forgiveness, but revenge. If someone hurts us, sometimes we just want them to stop, but often we want to get even or at least show them what they did to us.

There is an interesting connection between the passage and Genesis 4:24. Where Peter is told he must forgive seventy-seven times, in Genesis 4:24 we read that Lamech takes revenge on his enemy and comments, "If Cain is avenged seven times, then Lamech seventy-seven times." Jesus' command to offer unlimited forgiveness stands in stark contrast to Lamech's desire for unlimited revenge.[31] The Old Testament allowed for retaliation equal to the offense. In discussing the punishment for someone who injures a pregnant woman, Exodus 21:23–25, known as the lex talionis, states the principle as "life for life, eye for eye, tooth for tooth, hand for hand, foot for foot, burn for burn, wound for wound, bruise for bruise."

But the lex talionis was to be applied by civil authorities and not individuals. Rather than justifying revenge, its intent was actually to

---

28. Blomberg, *Preaching the Parables*, 73.

29. Gary Inrig, *The Parables: Understanding What Jesus Meant* (Grand Rapids: Discovery House, 1991), 68.

30. Inrig, *Parables*, 64.

31. Wenham, *Parables of Jesus*, 154.

prevent inappropriate retaliation by the offended parties. God's people were to leave justice to the authorities and not seek personal retribution. Instead, they were to love and serve each other.[32] Leviticus 19:18 states, "Do not seek revenge or bear a grudge against anyone among your people, but love your neighbor as yourself." This was to be the attitude of Jesus' disciples: "The obligation of [Jesus'] disciples is not first to retaliate for the evil done to them or to protect themselves and their personal interests. Their primary obligation is to serve those around them, both those who seem to deserve it and even those who don't."[33]

But Jesus' words about forgiveness do not mean that God is against justice. The people who *personally* forgave Dylann Roof in Charleston also recognized that there is a place for earthly justice for his crime. We must remember that God is a God of both mercy and justice. In Numbers 14:18 we read, "Yet he does not leave the guilty unpunished" (also Exod 34:7). At the same time, God is not impulsive and vengeful, but rather "slow to anger, abounding in love and forgiving sin and rebellion" (Num 14:18; also Exod 34:6). The biggest example of God's justice and mercy is his sending Christ to die for us on the cross. God's justice is maintained, and in a way that we can receive his mercy.

But what about when it is too difficult to forgive? What do you do when you know you need to obey, but your heart doesn't match the words in your mouth? What do you do when you find that you can't forgive?

Corrie ten Boom, who was imprisoned in a Nazi concentration camp during World War II for sheltering Jews, tells a remarkable story about forgiveness, illustrating how it is often something that can only come from God himself. During a church service in Munich after her release, she saw one of the former SS guards from the camp. Seeing him

---

32. Wilkins, *Matthew*, 248–49.
33. Wilkins, *Matthew*, 251.

brought back painful memories from the camp, memories of humiliation, degradation, and suffering for her and her sister, who died in the camp.

After the service the guard approached her, holding out his hand, saying, "How grateful I am for your message, *Fraulein*. To think, as you say, He has washed my sins away!"[34] Anger swept over her, and she was unable to forgive him. Finally, she prayed for Christ to forgive her and help her forgive him. She took his hand, and to her amazement she was filled with an almost overwhelming love for him. She concluded, "I discovered that it is not on our forgiveness any more than on our goodness that the world's healing hinges, but on His. When He tells us to love our enemies, He gives, along with the command, the love itself."[35]

In terms of forgiveness, as with all else the Lord calls us to do, he has not left us on our own. After all, our inability to live as we ought is what caused his sacrifice for us in the first place. Having been forgiven, we cannot assume that a blank sheet, a do-over, is all we need to live a life pleasing to God. As ten Boom noted, God's commands also come with a promise that he will enable us to follow them.

CONCLUSION: GOD, FORGIVENESS, AND US

What God gives is not simply the command, but also the means. Consider these parts of Scripture that tell us that what God has given us is Christ himself.

---

34. Corrie ten Boom with John and Elizabeth Sherrill, *The Hiding Place* (Washington Depot, CT: Chosen Books, 1971), 215.

35. Ten Boom, *Hiding Place*, 215.

- Romans 8:10: "But if Christ is in you, then even though your body is subject to death because of sin, the Spirit gives life because of righteousness."
- 1 Corinthians 1:30: "You are in Christ Jesus."
- 2 Corinthians 13:5: "Do you not realize that Christ Jesus is in you?"
- Galatians 2:20: "I have been crucified with Christ and I no longer live, but Christ lives in me."
- Ephesians 3:16–17: "I pray that out of his glorious riches he may strengthen you with power through his Spirit in your inner being, so that Christ may dwell in your hearts through faith."
- Colossians 1:27: "God has chosen to make known among the Gentiles the glorious riches of this mystery, which is Christ in you, the hope of glory."

While scholars debate what it means for Christ to be "in" us, one thing seems apparent. Following Jesus is more than simply following a good example. The life of Christ himself is in us. The one through whom I am forgiven is the one who enables me to forgive.

I wonder what would happen if I thought of forgiveness not simply as something I'm supposed to do (and which I do badly), but rather as a letting Christ in me? I've come to the conclusion that it doesn't work well to grit my teeth and make myself forgive, but maybe as I relate more to the King, I can comprehend what it means to give kingdom forgiveness, and God himself can help me forgive.

MAJOR TAKEAWAYS

1. The parable should be understood in the context of Peter's question of how often he should forgive. Jesus wants to change Peter's perspective from quantifying forgiveness to dwelling on the lavishness of God's forgiveness and how that changes us.

2. The parable does not teach that someone can "lose their salvation" or that God desires to torture people who do not forgive. Rather, it shows the seriousness of forgiveness and what God has already done for us.

3. God's forgiveness is based on his great compassion for us. It is not something that he does grudgingly or under compulsion.

4. Forgiveness is to be a defining characteristic of the people of God, a community of Christ's followers who extend compassion and grace to one another.

5. God's mercy does not invalidate God's justice. Rather God's justice leads to his mercy on us.

6. We cannot forgive on our own. The life of Christ himself dwelling in us can empower us to forgive.

QUESTIONS

1. What is your response to the first servant? What factors do you think cause you to respond in the way you do?

2. Whom do you need to forgive? What makes it difficult to forgive this person? How can you invite the Spirit to walk with you as you seek to forgive?

3. How do you think forgiveness might affect the person who forgives? The person who is forgiven?

4. What do you think it would look like if Christian communities practiced forgiveness toward one another? In what ways might it transform your community?

5. Do you think that God forgives you because of his great compassion for you? Why or why not? If you don't think so, how would it affect you if you did believe this?

TRUSTING IN THE GOD OF GRACE

*THE PARABLE OF THE FRIEND
AT MIDNIGHT (LUKE 11:5–13)*

Then he said to them, "Suppose one of you has a friend, and he goes to him at midnight and says, 'Friend, lend me three loaves of bread, because a friend of mine on a journey has come to me, and I have nothing to set before him.'

"Then the one inside answers, 'Don't bother me. The door is already locked, and my children are with me in bed. I can't get up and give you anything.' I tell you, though he will not get up and give him the bread because he is his friend, yet because of the man's boldness he will get up and give him as much as he needs.

"So I say to you: Ask and it will be given to you; seek and you will find; knock and the door will be opened to you. For everyone who asks receives; he who seeks finds; and to him who knocks, the door will be opened.

"Which of you fathers, if your son asks for a fish, will give him a snake instead? Or if he asks for an egg, will give him a scorpion? If you then, though you are *evil, know how to give good gifts to your children, how much more will your Father in heaven give the Holy Spirit to those who ask him!"* (NIV 1984)

INTRODUCTION

What are some things you can *really* count on? For example, I can count on my good friends to be there when I need them. I know that if I need to talk about something, they are more than willing to listen.

I also know I can depend on the people I work with. This gives me an enormous amount of security. If I have a problem, I know I can tell my bosses and they will help me with it. They aren't just waiting around to fire me if I make a mistake. They want me to succeed.

I also know some things I can't count on, such as money. Unexpected emergencies, stock-market slumps, and raises that don't come or just don't seem big enough remind me that it is foolish to place my hopes in money. Likewise, I can't count on always having good health. A severe case of the flu is a vivid reminder of the weakness of my body!

We base a good part of our lives on what we think we can or can't depend on, whether it's a car that we think may or may not get us to work, a friend we know will keep her promise and come through with what we need, or even choosing our favorite brand of bread at the grocery store because we know it will be good. Think about it. It's important to know what or whom we can trust, and we try to fill our lives with people and things we can trust. Life just seems to work better that way.

What are our thoughts on trusting God? How much do we really trust him? Why do we trust him? If we trust just because we know we're supposed to and we feel guilty if we don't, then we will find (as I have) that trust is not very sturdy. But if we trust because we know he is trustworthy, then it is easier to find that "peace of God, which transcends all understanding" (Phil 4:7). The parable of the friend at midnight teaches us that God is that trustworthy God.

THE PARABLE

The basic points of the parable are simple enough. A visitor arrives at a man's house. It is midnight, and the host does not have anything to serve him after his journey. The host goes to a friend's house to ask whether he will lend him three loaves of bread. However, the friend rejects the request, telling him not to bother him. He says to the man that the door is already shut and his children are in bed. Therefore, he cannot get up and give him anything. However, in the end he gives in. The parable says that because of the man's "boldness," the friend will get up and give him all that he needs.

THE CONTEXT OF HOSPITALITY

In the world of the first-century Jews, hospitality to travelers was an extremely valued tradition.[1] It was particularly important during this time because of the well-known reputation of most inns as places to be avoided if at all possible. The filthy sleeping areas were filled with insects and rodents, innkeepers often extorted travelers, and thieves often preyed on them. In addition, many inns were essentially brothels.[2]

---

1. We see hospitality in numerous places throughout Scripture. The first place it appears is in Gen 18, where Abraham welcomes strangers. Through them God then reveals that he will soon fulfill his promise of a child for Abraham and Sarah. Hospitality is characterized by mutual goodwill. When Jesus sends out his disciples, the expectation is that they will be the recipients of hospitality in their journeys (Luke 9:1–4; 10:1–9). The early Christian communities are expected to show hospitality (Rom 12:13; Heb 13:2; 1 Pet 4:9). See "Hospitality," in *The Baker Illustrated Bible Dictionary*, ed. Tremper Longman III (Grand Rapids: Baker, 2013), 808.

2. Everett Ferguson, *Backgrounds of Early Christianity*, 2nd ed. (Grand Rapids: Eerdmans, 1993), 81–82.

Hospitality was an important alternative to inns.[3] It would have been inconceivable not to receive travelers into your home, no matter what time of day. Because of the late hour, the man would have had difficulty providing for his guest.[4] Nevertheless, even then the obligations of hospitality remained. To receive someone, even if the person was a stranger, was considered a sacred responsibility.

Because the man does not have bread, he goes to his friend's house. Since it is late, he does not knock on the door, but instead calls him. He expects that his friend will recognize his voice and promptly open the door and help him. However, he does not help, at least not at first.[5]

Some have considered his actions reasonable. His house was most likely a very small one with only one room. During the day, it would be the family's living room, and at night their bedroom. In order to get up, the man would have to remove a bulky wooden bar that ran across the door. The family would be sleeping next to one another on the floor on mats. If the neighbor got up to let the man in, he would likely wake up the small children, who would cry and not be able to get to sleep again easily.[6]

---

3. Because of these dangers, hospitality played an important part in the early Christian community in meeting the needs of missionaries and other traveling believers. Ferguson, *Early Christianity*, 82.

4. Scholars are divided as to how common it would be for travelers to arrive at that late time. Some say that people normally traveled during the day because it would be too dangerous to travel at night; see J. Dwight Pentecost, *The Parables of Jesus* (Grand Rapids: Zondervan, 1982), 73. Others contend that because people would travel at night in order to avoid the extreme heat, it was unusual for someone to arrive so late; see Kenneth E. Bailey, *Poet & Peasant and Through Peasant Eyes*, combined ed. (Grand Rapids: Eerdmans, 1983), 121. At any rate, the point is that the host did not have bread and the late hour meant it would be difficult for him to obtain it since shops were closed for the evening and bread was baked to meet specific daily needs. See Darrell L. Bock, *Luke 9:51–24:53, Baker Exegetical Commentary on the New Testament* (Grand Rapids: Baker, 1996), 1057.

5. Brad H. Young, *The Parables: Jewish Tradition and Christian Interpretation* (Grand Rapids: Baker, 1998), 45.

6. Frederick W. Danker, *Jesus and the New Age* (Philadelphia: Fortress, 1988), 230; Pentecost, *Parables of Jesus*, 73.

Considering the trouble he would have to go through, we might be able to see why the friend could be reluctant to get up. But to the first-century Jew, to whom hospitality was of utmost importance, these would be lame excuses and completely unacceptable. To the shock of the first-century reader, he does not give the man what he needs.

The friend is not unable to help the man as much as he is unwilling. Jesus knows this when he prefaces the parable with the question, "Which of you who has a friend … ?" (Luke 11:5 ESV). The expected response to his rhetorical question would be "No one!" According to the conventions of hospitality, the friend's actions are inconceivable. One author says the question can be understood as, "Can you imagine having a guest and going to a neighbor to borrow bread and the neighbor offers ridiculous excuses about a locked door and sleeping children?"[7] Nevertheless, he violates the custom of hospitality and only gives in because of the man's "boldness" and not because of their friendship.

THE LESSON OF THE PARABLE

This parable is puzzling for several reasons. We wonder why the man does not get up to help his friend. More important, though, is the fact that he eventually gives in only because of the man's persistence. In other words, it sounds like he only helps in order to get rid of his pesky friend. This leads to perhaps the most important question: Does this mean that God only answers us when we become too annoying to ignore, rather than out of love and care?

In answering these questions, we can keep several things in mind. To begin with, the passage must be read in context. We can note that in the passage immediately before the parable, the disciples ask Jesus to tell them how to pray, and he answers by giving the Lord's Prayer

---

7. Bailey, *Poet & Peasant*, 119.

(Luke 11:1–4). In this prayer the disciples are instructed to pray for three things: (1) daily bread, (2) forgiveness of sins, and (3) not to be led into temptation.[8]

The prayer covers both material and spiritual needs. We are told that God will provide for our daily food. Just as Israel relied on God to provide them their manna day by day when they wandered in the wilderness, so will God honor this request by those who follow Christ. In addition to this material provision, the disciples are told to pray for their spiritual need in the forgiveness of their sins. This is not because they deserve it, but because God is gracious and also because they are willing to forgive in turn. As God shows mercy to them, they are also able to extend mercy to others. Third, they are to pray for spiritual protection, recognizing their dependence on God so they will not fall into temptation.

Jesus' prayer is short but direct. The disciples can ask for these things because God is their Father. What does it mean for God to be our Father? The term used here is "Abba," which conveyed both authority and intimacy.[9] It is a term of warmth that children used of their earthly fathers in the context of their secure and loving care.[10] It carries both the sense of our relationship with God and his ability to guide and protect us. This is the Father we are to pray to (Luke 11:2) and the one who gives to those who ask (Luke 11:13). The parable of the friend at midnight follows this teaching in order to reveal more about what it means to pray to the Father.

We can then go to what follows the parable, where Jesus tells us more about the Father and prayer:

---

8. Luke's version of the Lord's Prayer is slightly different from the one in Matt 6:9–13. For example, the prayer in Luke omits "your will be done, on earth as it is in heaven" (Matt 6:10b) and "but deliver us from the evil one" (Matt 6:13).

9. Bock, *Luke 9:51–24:53*, 1051.

10. Michael J. Wilkins, *Matthew, NIV Application Commentary* (Grand Rapids: Zondervan, 2004), 273.

So I say to you: Ask and it will be given to you; seek and you will find; knock and the door will be opened to you. For everyone who asks receives; the one who seeks finds; and to the one who knocks, the door will be opened.

Which of you fathers, if your son asks for a fish, will give him a snake instead? Or if he asks for an egg, will give him a scorpion? If you then, though you are evil, know how to give good gifts to your children, how much more will your Father in heaven give the Holy Spirit to those who ask him! (Luke 11:9–13)

Jesus explains that we can be confident in the Father's answers to prayer, for the one who asks will receive. This is God's promise to us, and we can be assured of this because of who God is.

Jesus uses a rabbinic form of argument that reasons, if something is true in a lesser instance, "how much more" will that be the case in a greater instance. If even we who are "evil"—or even a friend who does not act like a friend —will help, how much more will your perfect heavenly Father give good things to his children? This is why God's children can present their prayers with boldness to the Father.[11]

---

11. Sometimes people think the main point of the parable is the need to be persistent, as in the parable of the persistent widow and the unjust judge in Luke 18:1–8. In that parable a widow seeks justice from a judge against her opponent. While he initially refuses, he eventually gives in because of her persistence. Luke records the man's reasoning: "Though I neither fear God nor respect man, yet because this widow keeps bothering me, I will give her justice, so that she will not beat me down by her continual coming"(ESV). The lesson is that if even an unrighteous judge will give justice to the widow who demonstrates such perseverance, will not God also give justice to the ones "who cry to him day and night?" (Luke 18:7 ESV).

Although there is certainly a quality of the man's persistence in the parable of the friend at midnight, the emphasis is slightly different. The NIV says it is because of the man's "boldness" that the friend gives him what he needs. Although

However, it is important to remember that God will give his children the good things *that he has promised them*. It is not up to us to determine what these good things are, but to trust that our heavenly Father intends good for us. But very often, the good that we want is not the same as the good that he provides, and that can be hard to accept.

RESPONDING TO THE PARABLE

How hard is it to trust that God will give us truly good things? At times, impossibly hard. In her books, Christian author Kara Tippetts describes her heartbreaking battle with breast cancer. She writes about what she learned from her cancer, such as appreciating the small moments, focusing on what is truly important, and needing Christ's strength through the pain and trauma of her treatment. She mourns for all of the things she will miss—time with her husband, watching her young children grow up. She also speaks of trust. She is not afraid to die, but struggles with leaving her husband and children behind and what their lives will be like without her. However, she trusts that God in his grace will provide for them.

> As our story continues to struggle, and the plot of
> my cancer thickens, God has deepened our love,

---

some translations, such as the NASB and the NRSV, say "persistence," others more correctly bring out the brazenness of the man's behavior. Similar to the NIV, the ESV describes what the man does as "impudence."

Why are these better ways to describe what the man did? Although the friend shockingly refuses to open the door, the man knows the situation is critical enough that he has to have that bread. As Young states, "A person with brazen tenacity demands what he or she requires without shame" (*Parables*, 49). He will do whatever is necessary in order to get what he needs.

Even more than persistence, the man demonstrates a boldness in demanding what he needs. The lesson of the parable of the friend at midnight is different from that of the persistent widow, which is that God's children "should always pray and not give up" (Luke 18:1). In the friend at midnight, persistence is present, but the emphasis is more on the boldness of the one in need.

helped us in our weakness to begin to have an imagination for heaven, and met us in such gentle grace where we cling. I picture God's gentle countenance as I beg for more time, more loving, more enjoying the crumbs, as I can't see the next season in all its fullness. I don't struggle with dying, but I struggle and lose my breath when I think of my family watching me suffer through finding my way to heaven. I struggle as I will see my pain reflected in their faces. I will see their fears in letting me go, and knowing the graces that will follow.[12]

Tippetts doesn't know what these graces will look like but trusts that they will be there when needed most. In speaking of her concern for her husband, she writes: "But I know, I quietly know, when the time comes for that last breath to take place, a beautiful grace will meet my dear love in that sacred moment. What seems utterly frightening and lonely will be a moment filled with grace and peace. We cannot know it, because that grace has yet to come, but I believe it will be there."[13]

Perhaps this is the hardest element of trust, the not knowing. The knowing somehow feels more concrete, gives us something we can picture and hold on to. But God has not asked us to trust in something, but in someone: himself.

Paul describes how he wrestled with accepting God's will in his life and trusting that God was truly providing him with what he most needed. In 2 Corinthians 12:7–10, he describes his battle against what he calls his "thorn in my flesh." Although we don't know exactly what this thorn was, it is clear that it was something that caused him a

---

12. Kara Tippetts, *The Hardest Peace: Expecting God's Grace in the Midst of Life's Hard* (Colorado Springs: David C. Cook, 2014), 105.

13. Tippetts, *Hardest Peace*, 107–8.

lot of distress, since he says its effect was to "torment" him.[14] Paul begged three times for the Lord to take the thorn from him, but he didn't. Eventually Paul realized that what he needed was not for God to remove the thorn, but to provide grace in the midst of his pain. Paul didn't get relief from the thorn, but he did gain strength from allowing God to work through his weakness. This experience meant so much to him that he says he learned to "delight" in his weaknesses and difficulties (2 Cor 12:10).

If Paul had to struggle to learn this lesson, then this gives me hope for myself. What is difficult for me to learn is that I may not have the grace to trust now, but that I have to trust that God will give the grace when needed, if I am faithful to step out because of who he is.

As with the other parables, we are called to respond personally to the story. Since the passage begins with the rhetorical question, "Which one of you ... ?" Jesus' audience would individualize the question and identify with the man who goes calling on his friend.[15] The question calls us to consider that just as it is inconceivable in the first-century Jewish culture that someone would refuse someone's request for help in providing hospitality, even more so is it impossible that the Father would not want to give his children good things.

Do you believe that God wants to give you good things? While the parable tells us to pray with boldness, this is not something we can just do on our own, as if we can will ourselves to have more faith. Rather, Jesus challenges us to know who God is, that he is good and that he desires our good, and then to pray in the security of that knowledge.

---

14. There has been much discussion on what the thorn might be. Some see it as a physical problem, such as a disease or disfigurement. Others see it as relational, such as some type of opposition or persecution. For a brief summary and discussion of the options, see Paul Barnett, *The Second Epistle to the Corinthians*, New International Commentary on the New Testament (Grand Rapids: Eerdmans, 1997), 569–70.

15. Arland J. Hultgren, *The Parables of Jesus* (Grand Rapids: Eerdmans, 2000), 228.

Therefore, in order to respond well to the parable, we need to understand deeply who our heavenly Father is.

OUR TRUSTWORTHY GOD

Jesus explains that God's children can ask of the Father precisely because he wants to give them good things. If even the selfish friend can be persuaded to give the man what he needs, *how much more* will the one who created us give us good things. In the same way, even human fathers, whom Jesus calls "evil," will give good gifts to their children. If this is the case, *how much more* can we expect from our loving, all-knowing, and all-powerful heavenly Father!

Even the best human father is sinful (Rom 3:23) and ungodly (Rom 5:6). But consider what Scripture says about how wonderful God the Father is and how different he is from even the best earthly father.

- He is the one who takes care of our most basic physical needs because he considers us valuable (Matt 6:25–34).
- He is the one who sustains the entire world, causing the sun to rise and sending rain on everyone, even those who do not acknowledge him (Matt 5:45).
- He is the one we can cast all our cares on because he will sustain us (Ps 55:22).
- He is the one who makes our paths straight (Prov 3:5).
- He is the one we can trust, because he never forsakes those who seek him (Ps 9:10).
- He is the one who promises to give us true peace (John 14:27).
- He is the one we can cast all our anxiety on, because he cares for us (1 Pet 5:7).

- He is the one who sent Christ to die for us, even while we were his "enemies," "sinners," and "ungodly" (Rom 5:6–10).

If very imperfect, sinful human fathers can bless their children, what can we expect from God? In this parable, we learn that God will provide generously to meet his people's needs. We learn that God is not a remote and distant God, but one who is intimately involved in his people's smallest, most trivial and deepest, most meaningful concerns. And we learn that he does not want his children to be the slightest bit hesitant to bring their needs to him. We know that he looks after all our needs, that we can trust him completely, and that his love for us never fails, even when we fail him.

CONCLUSION: TRUSTING THE FATHER

I remember the warm feeling of safety when I would ride in the car with my parents when I was growing up. It might be intensely dark outside as we traveled on a lonely road, but I felt secure in the back seat knowing my parents would make sure we got home. I never questioned whether I would have a place to sleep at night, just as I never questioned whether I would have my next meal, clothes to wear, or presents at my next birthday. I realize that I grew up very privileged, since not all children have this security. Nor were my parents perfect. But I *felt* secure. We all crave that sense of safety, that things will be provided for us, that someone will give us good things.

We were created to trust, and when that sense of trust is violated, it is devastating. We need to know that we can trust someone, that others want good for us, and that they will give good for us. To varying degrees, we may experience this from our friends and family, perhaps even strangers. But none of this can compare to what we can expect to receive from our Father. James 1:17 states, "Every good and perfect gift is from above, coming down from the Father of the heavenly lights, who does not change like shifting shadows." The only true good comes from the one who is truly good. He is also trustworthy because he does not change in his goodness. Therefore, we can feel secure because we *are* secure.

Yet it is also important to consider what we are trusting God for. We tend to focus on God's provision for our material needs. In the Lord's Prayer we are told to pray for our "daily bread." Jesus in the Sermon on the Mount reassures us not to worry about what we will eat, drink, or wear (Matt 6:25–34). But the point of this particular parable is our spiritual needs. The parable does not give believers a blank check to request whatever they want, as if we could expect God to give us a new sports car or a fancy house, but a promise of abundance—for all of our spiritual needs. What we can't miss is that at the very end of Jesus' explanation, he clarifies that what the Father will give is the Holy Spirit.

It is through the Spirit that we receive the promises of God. The Spirit is the one who guides us (John 16:13), teaches us (John 14:26), and gives us peace (Rom 8:6), hope (Rom 15:13), love (Rom 5:5), wisdom (1 Cor 2:6–16), and courage (Acts 4:31). He is the one who intercedes for us (Rom 8:26–27) and gives us life (John 3:5). For most people, it is harder to think about the Holy Spirit than God the Father or God the Son. But the New Testament tells us that the Holy Spirit is not some mysterious, impersonal force, but rather the Spirit of God himself (1 Cor 2:12). He is the one who gives us God's blessings. As wonderful as material blessings can be, how much more is what we can have through the Spirit. He is the one who enables me to live under God's grace when what I usually prefer is to whine, be resentful, and worry.

I wonder, though, how much we pray for these spiritual blessings. I pray often that God would help me in certain situations. But when I really think about it, am I praying for peace through the Spirit or for God to fix the situation so that I can experience not peace, but the removal of a problem? Am I praying for God to solve my worldly problem or to give me his Spirit so that I can bring good to the situation? Do I pray that God would help me to love my enemies (Matt 5:44), or do I want God to change my enemies so that they will somehow end up liking and agreeing with me? I wonder whether I've gotten things mixed up so that somehow I think that worldly blessing is spiritual blessing, when perhaps I've misunderstood from the beginning what is really "good." I want to believe Romans 8:28, which says that "all things work together for the good of those who love him," and like to gloss over the next verse, which says the good being worked in my life is "to be conformed to the image of his Son," who suffered and died on my behalf because God loves me.

So here is a truth that puts things in perspective for me. If I fret about material, earthly things, I lose sight of spiritual good. But if I have peace in my spirit, I can trust God to provide for all of my needs. I remember Christ's words in the Sermon on the Mount that why should I worry about what I will eat, or drink, or wear, when I already see how God takes care of the birds of the air? But if I "seek first his kingdom and his righteousness," then "all these things will be given" to me (Matt 6:25–33). This shows me what I should really be more concerned about. Life is often difficult, but I can trust that a loving, caring Father will get me home safely.

MAJOR TAKEAWAYS

1. The man could expect help from his friend because of the custom of hospitality. His initial refusal is a serious offense, even though he had reasons not to

respond. Eventually, though, he relents because of the man's boldness.

2. We can be bold in our prayers because the Father desires to give good things to his children.

3. If even sinful human fathers desire to give good things to their children, we can expect our perfect heavenly Father to give much more to his children.

4. In order to trust that God desires to give us good things, we need to know that God himself is good.

5. The good that God gives his children is not just material good, but spiritual good in the giving of the Holy Spirit so we can be conformed to Christ's image.

QUESTIONS

1. What do you think are the "good things" God wants to give his children? What is one area in your life in which you are currently having difficulty trusting that God will give you good things?

2. Do you ever think that God is like the reluctant friend, only answering prayers because he has to and doesn't want to be bothered anymore? Why do you think you believe this?

3. What does it mean to pray to God as Father in the biblical sense? How would it affect your prayers to think of God in this way?

4. What do you think bold and persistent prayer looks like? What keeps you from praying in this way?

5. Can you think of a time when you trusted God even when you didn't know what his grace would look like? What happened, and how has that shaped your faith?

6. What "good things" from the Spirit do you need in your life at this moment? Can you boldly present those needs to the Father right now?

SERVING THE GOD OF GRACE

Again, it will be like a man going on a journey, who called his servants and entrusted his wealth to them. To one he gave five bags of gold [talents], to another two bags [talents], and to another one bag [talent], each according to his ability. Then he went on his journey. The man who had received five bags of gold went at once and put his money to work and gained five bags more. So also, the one with two bags of gold gained two more. But the man who had received one bag went off, dug a hole in the ground and hid his master's money.

After a long time the master of those servants returned and settled accounts with them. The man who had received five bags of gold brought the other five. "Master," he said, "you entrusted me with five bags of gold. See, I have gained five more."

His master replied, "Well done, good and faithful servant! You have been faithful with a few things; I will put you in charge of many things. Come and share your master's happiness!"

The man with two bags of gold also came. "Master," he said, "you entrusted me with two bags of gold; see, I have gained two more."

His master replied, "Well done, good and faithful servant! You have been faithful with a few things; I will put you in charge of many things. Come and share your master's happiness!"

Then the man who had received one bag of gold came. "Master," he said, "I knew that you are a hard man, harvesting where you have not sown and gathering where you have not scattered seed. So I was afraid and went out and hid your gold in the ground. See, here is what belongs to you."

His master replied, "You wicked, lazy servant! So you knew that I harvest where I have not sown and gather where I have not scattered seed? Well then, you should have put my money on deposit with the bankers, so that when I returned I would have received it back with interest.

"So take the gold from him and give it to the one who has ten bags. For whoever has will be given more, and they will have an abundance. Whoever does not have, even what they have will be taken from them. And throw that worthless servant outside, into the darkness, where there will be weeping and gnashing of teeth."

INTRODUCTION

The Christian life can be confusing sometimes—well, oftentimes. Just take serving, for instance. I know I am supposed to serve, but how am I supposed to serve? For example, as a member of my church, I have Bible studies to teach and attend, church functions to take part in, and people to meet and minister to. There are also a multitude of other ministries to participate in, from missions trips to service to the homeless to helping with parking on Sunday morning. There are also many expectations in my role as a professor. I am to teach my classes, serve on committees, write books, and mentor students. But how many students am I supposed to mentor? Do I need to say "yes" every time I am asked to be a part of a committee? How carefully should I grade all of those papers? Even just thinking about all of this can be quite exhausting, but isn't service what the Christian life is about?

Right now, I am on a research leave from my school, meaning that I am excused from teaching and committee duties for a semester to write this book. During this time, I've noticed something interesting. While writing a book can be a lot of work, it does not demand the constant pace that I find myself in during the regular school year. During the school year, it seems like the days and weeks blend into one another, with my primary thoughts often circling around how I can get everything done.

Now that I'm not constantly busy, I've found myself with some different kinds of thoughts. I pay more attention to my husband and our two dogs. I've become a bit more creative with what I make for dinner. I'm generally in a better mood, which means I have a little more patience, even to the customer service representatives I talk with on the phone, even when they put me on hold for forty-five minutes and ask me to repeat the same thing I just told the previous representative for whom I had to wait forty-five minutes. Even more, though, I've discovered that this time has given me the space to discover some more about what I really think, what I'm good at, and what I want to do and say, and that feels really good.

Each time I go on leave, it seems I learn a new lesson about my relationship with God. This time the lesson seems to revolve around the question, Am I paying attention to what I think God has called me to do, or am I getting caught up in the many "good" things that seem to demand my attention? Or perhaps another way to say it could be, Am I really serving to serve God, or for another reason, whether to make myself look/feel good, to avoid conflict, to avoid disappointing someone, and so on?

Now, this may seem like an odd introduction to the parable of the talents, in which two servants are commended for their productivity to the master, while the third servant is condemned for not doing anything. But the point of the parable is not simply about being productive. Instead, it is about being good stewards of what God has given us and being a effective servants because we understand the true character of God. In other words, it turns us away from simply trying to be productive and causes us to see that following Christ means being intimately acquainted with the master and paying attention to the resources—such as people, money, and skills—that he has blessed us with.

THE PARABLE

In Matthew's Gospel, Jesus tells a parable about a man going on a journey who entrusts three of his servants with various amounts of money. Two apparently use the money well and are rewarded. However, the third does not do anything with the money and is punished. Clearly, the parable teaches us about stewardship in some way, but what are the main lessons?

In the parable, the man gives one servant five talents, another two talents, and the last one talent. We learn that the money is apportioned to each "according to his ability." While the man is away, the first servant uses his money to gain five more talents. The second one puts his money to work also and increases his amount by another two talents. However, the third does not do anything with the money and instead hides it in a hole.

When the man comes back, he calls the servants to account for what they have done with the money. The servant who was given five talents reports that he has earned five more. The man commends the servant for his activity, calling him "good and faithful." Since he has been faithful in the "few things" that he was entrusted with, he will now be in charge of many things. The man ends his praise of the servant by inviting him to "Come and share your master's happiness!"

The man then calls the second servant, who reports that he has earned two more. He receives the same approval. The third servant, however, reports that he has not earned anything for the man because he hid his money. He tells the master that he did this because he was afraid of him, knowing that he is a "hard man, harvesting where you have not sown and gathering where you have not scattered seed" (Matt 25:24).

Rather than praise, the third servant receives condemnation. The man calls him a "wicked, lazy servant." Even if the master were that harsh, the servant should have at least invested the money with bankers to earn interest. Because the servant did not handle the money properly, the man orders his talent to be given to the one who now has ten talents, and for the unfaithful servant to be thrown outside into the darkness. The man states the principle behind his actions: "For whoever has will be given more, and they will have an abundance. Whoever does not have, even what they have will be taken from them."

How are we to respond to the parable of the talents? Are we to live in fear that we are not serving God properly and are in danger of being "thrown into the darkness"? What if we don't get results like the first two servants did? Does the parable teach us that God measures our faithfulness by how much we earn for him?

THE KINGDOM CONTEXT

It will be helpful to begin by setting the parable in its context. The passage comes toward the end of Matthew's Gospel, when Jesus teaches about the end times in what is known as the Olivet Discourse.[1] Jesus tells the disciples three parables after they ask when this will happen and what is the sign of Jesus' coming and the end of the age.

The theme of the parables is being prepared for Christ's return. He says his return will come at a time that people do not expect, like a thief who breaks into a house at night (Matt 24:42–44). Because of the unknown time of his return, people must be ready. The first parable tells the story of a servant put in charge of the household when his master is gone. In the first scenario, the servant acts responsibly. In the second, he thinks the master will be gone a long time and so begins to beat the other servants and spend time drunkenly with bad company. Throughout Scripture these types of actions are associated with idolaters and those who do not belong to or have fallen away from the faith.[2] When the master returns unexpectedly and sees what the servant has been doing, he condemns the servant (Matt 24:45–51).[3]

In the second parable, the parable of the ten virgins, the wise virgins bring oil in their jars along with their lamps in order to wait for the bridegroom.[4] The foolish ones do not. When the bridegroom takes a long time to arrive, the foolish ones have to go out to buy more oil.

---

1. The Olivet Discourse is found in Matt 24:1-25:46; Mark 13:1-37; and Luke 21:5-36.

2. For example, Exod 32:6; Isa 28:7; 1 Cor 10:7; Gal 5:21. See Michael J. Wilkins, *Matthew, NIV Application Commentary* (Grand Rapids: Zondervan, 2004), 803.

3. Specifically, we read in Matt 24:51, "He will cut him to pieces and assign him a place with the hypocrites, where there will be weeping and gnashing of teeth"!

4. The setting may reflect a typical scene from a marriage ceremony. The bridegroom and his friends would go to the bride's house for some ceremonies. This would be followed by a nighttime procession to his home in which everyone was to have his or her own light. See D. A. Carson, "Matthew," in *The Expositor's Bible Commentary*, gen. ed. Frank E. Gaebelein (Grand Rapids: Zondervan, 1984), 8:513.

While they are gone, they miss the bridegroom's return and are shut out of the wedding banquet (Matt 25:1–13).

All of the parables are set in the context of Christ's return. The first parable explains that God's people must be faithful in their responsibilities while they wait for his return during the delay. The second parable emphasizes that they must be ready since the time is unknown. The contribution of the parable of the talents is that God's people are to be productive in the meantime.[5]

The parables demonstrate that we have responsibilities. When we think about salvation, we often think about going to heaven after we die. But the Gospels make clear that what we do during our lifetime also matters—a lot. How should we think about this? What is our role now, and how does it relate to what awaits us in the future? For this, it is important to know how salvation involves our participation in the kingdom of God.

In the biblical perspective, we are living in what is known as the "already but not yet." Simply put, the Old Testament describes how God sought to establish his kingship through his people on earth to reflect his glory. Israel was commissioned to do this but failed. However, where Israel disobeyed, we read in the New Testament that Christ was faithful and succeeded, setting in motion his kingdom reign. But while Christ established the kingdom through his life, death, and resurrection, the kingdom will not be fully present until his second coming (e.g., 1 Thess 4:13–17). So we live in the in-between times, where the kingdom is "already" here at the same time it is "not yet" fully here. In the meantime, believers have received the Holy Spirit to live in them, as promised in John's Gospel (John 14:15–17), and to empower them, as described by Peter in Acts 2:14–18:

> Then Peter stood up with the Eleven, raised his
> voice and addressed the crowd: "Fellow Jews and

---

5. Wilkins, *Matthew*, 814–15.

all of you who live in Jerusalem, let me explain this to you; listen carefully to what I say. These men are not drunk, as you suppose. It's only nine in the morning! No, this is what was spoken by the prophet Joel:

'In the last days, God says,
   I will pour out my Spirit on all people.
Your sons and daughters will prophesy,
   your young men will see visions,
   your old men will dream dreams.
Even on my servants, both men and women,
   I will pour out my Spirit in those days,
   and they will prophesy.'"

God's people are called to be Spirit-empowered ministers and ambassadors to a still-fallen world. We are called to work for the kingdom. In this context, the parables teach us about our responsibilities while we wait for Christ's return. We are to be about the business of the kingdom, putting to use the resources God has given us, and to be prepared for him to return at any moment.

WHAT DID THE THIRD SERVANT DO WRONG?

We can examine the actions of the servants in this context. After the first two servants are commended by the master, the third servant is punished for his actions, or rather lack of action. Instead of using the money to earn more, he hid it in a hole, so that when the master returned, he could give him his money back, but without any gain.

There have been a number of interpretations about the significance of what the servant did. The servant explains he hid the money because he was afraid of the master since he is a hard man, "harvesting where you have not sown and gathering where you have not scattered seed" (Matt 25:24–25). Some think the servant was responding to an accurate characterization of the master, since the master apparently agrees with this description (Matt 25:26), and this would fit closely with that of a typical landowner in that day.[6]

Other scholars note that what the servant did was not that unusual or problematic. A popular rabbinic saying describes burying money as the surest way to safeguard it.[7] The Roman discovery of large underground stores of gold, silver, and other treasures after they conquered Jerusalem in AD 70 seems to reflect this practice.[8] Jesus even describes the kingdom of heaven as "like a treasure hidden in a field" (Matt 13:44). If this is the case and the master was also known as being severe, then the servant's actions would be seen as very reasonable.[9] He simply chose security over risk.[10]

The most important point may be that the servant misunderstood the master's character. He describes him as "a hard man, harvesting where you have not sown and gathering where you have not scattered seed." While the master affirms the latter part of what the servant says, he does not repeat or agree with the servant's charge that he is a "hard man" (Matt 25:24–26). The servant was fearful and so was unwilling to do anything with the master's money based on this erroneous

---

6. For example, Wright describes him as "representative of the landlord who gradually, through rents and taxes, accumulated the land of the peasants." Stephen Wright, *Tales Jesus Told: An Introduction to the Narrative Parables of Jesus* (Carlisle, UK: Paternoster, 2002), 145.

7. Babylonian Talmud Baba Metzia 42a, as cited in Craig L. Blomberg, *Interpreting the Parables* (Downers Grove, IL: InterVarsity, 1990), 215.

8. Arland J. Hultgren, *The Parables of Jesus* (Grand Rapids: Eerdmans, 2000), 275–76.

9. Blomberg, *Interpreting the Parables,* 215.

10. Hultgren, *Parables of Jesus,* 275.

perception, while the first two servants seem to trust that the master is good and were willing to take risks.[11]

In Judaism, one served God not out of fear, but out of love. It is important to note that the first commandment, "You shall have no other gods before me," includes a description of God as "showing love to a thousand generations of those who love me and keep my commandments" (Exod 20:3–6). Similarly, what is considered the most important prayer in Judaism, the Shema, emphasizes the importance of loving God.[12] Jesus himself says that the greatest commandment is to love God "with all your heart and with all your soul and with all your mind and with all your strength" (Mark 12:29–30; Matt 22:37–38; Luke 10:27).

Because the servant misunderstood God, he acted out of mistrust and fear, which led to laziness.[13] Moreover, he blames the master for his actions, something that the foolish virgins in the previous parable do not do (Matt 25:1–13).[14]

RESPONDING TO THE PARABLE

The sum each worker gets is enormous. In Jesus' day, a talent was a very large unit of currency, equal to six thousand denarii. If a denarii was one day's wage for a laborer, then one talent would be worth twenty years' wages, and five talents would be worth thirty thousand denarii, or one hundred years' wages![15]

---

11. Brad H. Young, *The Parables: Jewish Tradition and Christian Interpretation* (Grand Rapids: Baker, 1998), 82.

12. The title, Shema, is a transliteration of the Hebrew word for "hear." It comes from the first word in Deut 6:4, "Hear, O Israel ..." "Shema, The," in *Baker Illustrated Dictionary*, ed. Tremper Longman III (Grand Rapids: Baker, 2013), 1518.

13. Wilkins, *Matthew*, 807.

14. Carson, "Matthew," 517.

15. Assuming someone worked three hundred days out of the year (Hultgren, *Parables of Jesus*, 274–75).

Both of the first two servants double the master's money, the first earning an additional five talents to add to the original five, and the second two more from his first two. Although the parable describes how much each servant earns, the focus is not on the amount gained for the master. Both earn proportionately more from what was given to them, and each receives the same praise from the master.

Each servant is given responsibility for the money from the master, and each is accountable for what he does with it. The two faithful servants put their talent to work to gain something for the man. The third servant, based on his view of his master as harsh, does nothing.

The parable does not emphasize the magnitude of what one does as much as faithfulness with what one has been given. Responsible stewardship is what matters. The talents seem to represent the resources that God has given each believer.

What are the "talents" that Christians today have? It is probably best to see these resources not as a single kind, but the whole of what God may give someone, since God gives us a wide range of resources. The point is that we have been enabled by God to use what he gives us, and it is our responsibility to use all of it well.

We can consider what are all of the other resources we can use. Scripture also contains many passages about the "gifts" or supernatural endowments from the Spirit (Rom 12:6–8; 1 Cor 12:8–11, 28–30; Eph 4:11–12). Romans 12:6–8 gives us a sample list of what these gifts look like: "We have different gifts, according to the grace given to each of us. If your gift is prophesying, then prophesy in accordance with your faith; if it is serving, then serve; if it is teaching, then teach; if it is to encourage, then give encouragement; if it is giving, then give generously; if it is to lead, do it diligently; if it is to show mercy, do it cheerfully."

Think creatively about what you have to offer. What are some things you are able to do for others because you have more time than they might have? Can you give an encouraging word to someone who really looks like they could use it? Can you open up your home to someone who needs a place to stay, even if just for a few days? Are there students in your church who could use an "adopted" family while they are away from their own families? God has not given each of us the same things, but he has given us the same charge.

When we realize God expects faithfulness rather than success, it also takes a lot of pressure off. It is easy to think we are measured by how many people we bring to Christ, what kind of ministry we are doing and how many people respond positively to it, or what our family life looks like (or doesn't look like).

When I was hired at my school, I was the first woman hired to teach full time in the Bible department. While there were challenges to being the first, it wasn't too bad because my colleagues were very supportive and helpful. In fact, being the only woman had its own advantages. One was that I couldn't be compared negatively to anyone, since there wasn't anyone else to be compared to!

A few years later we hired another woman, and she has done a wonderful job. Her teaching evaluations are great, students love her, she publishes constantly, and she is continually asked to be on committees, give advice, and speak at conferences and retreats. While I very much enjoy having a female friend in my department, it sometimes is hard not to compare myself negatively with her. I've wondered, do people notice I don't get asked to do the things she gets asked to do? What do they think about how popular she is with the students compared with me? I thought I was doing okay, but do I look second- (or third-) rate compared with her? Why can't I be as cheerful as she?

It is frighteningly easy to compare myself with others. But I've begun to realize that I need to focus on the gifts and resources I've been given and to steward them well. No matter how many "talents" I've been given, God can use them, and it is my responsibility to make them available and be willing to put them to use.

While every believer receives spiritual gifts from the Holy Spirit (e.g., 1 Cor 12:7–11), Paul also makes clear that the same gifts are not given to everyone (1 Cor 12:29–20). That means that I should expect that I will be lacking in some areas (many areas!). I was not meant to be perfect, or superhuman, but I was created to love God and obey him.

Focusing on faithfulness, not results, is key. The prophets provide an important example. Were they successful? Well, Jeremiah obeys God in prophesying to the southern kingdom of Judah, warning them to repent or face God's judgment. If success is the measure of God's followers, then Jeremiah doesn't measure up very well. The nation does not repent, and Jeremiah himself is beaten, put in stocks, mocked, and ridiculed (Jer 20). In the end, the people do not listen to him and are sent into exile. For the most part, the prophets do not achieve a great deal of success in turning the people back to God. I suspect they know it is a lost cause from the moment they are called. But they are called to be faithful, and they are. They obey God and also leave the results up to God. How can we not do the same?

Our culture tells us to measure ourselves by tangible pieces of evidence that we are doing "well"—things that can be counted, measured, and compared. Scripture tells us that obedience and loving God are what matters. The Christians we hear about are the ones who pastor megachurches, write best-selling books, or are continually interviewed on TV. We rarely hear about the people who minister faithfully in small churches, pray continually in their personal prayer closets, or simply serve the next needy person who comes their way. But these are the foot soldiers of God's army, and they make up the substance of God's people.

But even if I want to console myself that it's okay not to be as great as the people I compare myself with, the key point is that I am not the point. God has created me to contribute to the whole body of Christ

(1 Cor 12). First Peter 4:10 reminds me that I am to use what I have been given to serve others. God has not given me talents, gifts, and other resources to make me feel good about myself but to help bring others to wholeness and to help them be faithful disciples.

While the parable seems to stress the results of what the servants did, the more important point is seen in the master's commendation of the first two. He calls them "good and faithful," not "smart and successful." Their reward is to "come and share your master's happiness!" not "receive much applause in front of a huge crowd." We are to evaluate the worth and effectiveness of what we do not in relation to other people, but in relation to God.

CONCLUSION: SERVING THE KING

Seeing God as Creator and connecting that to our role as caretakers of his creation was central to the Jewish mindset. One's view of God profoundly impacted one's stewardship.[16] The third servant's view of God as hard causes him to be fearful. We are not explicitly told what the other two servants think. But they are contrasts to the third servant and apparently felt free to take risks with the master's money.[17]

It is critical to see that much of what we do comes from our view of God. Do you see God as kind, loving, and forgiving? Or do you see him as harsh and vindictive? Think of how each view affects how you respond. Moreover, what do you see as your relationship with him? Is God simply there to fulfill your needs, get you out of trouble, and give you a happy/comfortable life? Or do you see following Christ as the opportunity to serve the God who saved you, to take part in the

---

16. Young, *Parables*, 82.

17. Giving money to the three servants sets up what is called the "rule of three" in storytelling, in which the third servant is the "object of scorn or derision" (Hultgren, *Parables of Jesus*, 275). The first two are "good and faithful" as opposed to the "wicked, lazy" servant. They were the ones who judge the master correctly and act properly.

kingdom and what God is doing to redeem the world? It is good to realize that "Faithfulness is contingent on an accurate view of God."[18]

Our view of God and our view of the Christian life are intimately intertwined. Paul tells us that we can consider ourselves children of God, and God as our Father. Indeed, the Holy Spirit resides deep within us and cries out to the Father, as Paul tells us in Galatians 4:6. "Because you are his sons, God sent the Spirit of his Son into our hearts, the Spirit who calls out, 'Abba, Father.'"

And Paul says that because of this we are not slaves, but sons (Gal 4:7), and so we are invited to share in the kingdom work of our Father.

How we think of the Christian life matters. It is not up to us to determine how much we are to do, but to recognize what we have been given and serve faithfully with what we have. We are not to use others as the standard for what we do or don't do, but are called to eagerly join with what God is doing.

There is a famous story associated with Christopher Wren, the great architect who designed St. Paul's Cathedral. As he walked unrecognized among the men working on the building, he asked one man, "What are you doing?" to which the man replied, "I am cutting a piece of stone." He asked the same of the second man, and he replied, "I am earning five shillings twopence a day." When he offered the question to the third man, he answered, "I am helping Sir Christopher Wren build a beautiful cathedral."[19] He knew he was participating in something magnificent, and Christ invites us to participate in the larger kingdom work that he is doing.

---

18. He goes on to explain in regard to the servant, "The parable reveals that the wickedness of the servant impelled him to pervert the image of his master, which then provided him with an excuse for his personal irresponsibility" (Wilkins, *Matthew*, 7).

19. Attributed to Louise Bush-Brown, reported as unverified in *Respectfully Quoted: A Dictionary of Quotations* (Washington, DC: Library of Congress, 1989).

MAJOR TAKEAWAYS

1. God gives believers gifts and resources, but each is given a different share.
2. God calls his children to faithful stewardship of what he has given them.
3. God desires faithfulness more than "success."
4. The third servant is negligent in his stewardship because he has a mistaken view of God. Our view of God affects our discipleship, including whether we serve God out of love or something else, such as fear or obligation.
5. Comparing ourselves with others can hinder our faithfulness, putting the focus on us and what we do, rather than on God.

QUESTIONS

1. In what ways are you like the first two servants? Why?
2. In what ways are you like the third servant? Why?
3. When you first read the parable, what is your reaction to the master and the way he treats the third servant? Why do you think you react in this way, and what does your reaction reveal about how you think about God and the Christian life?
4. In what ways do you believe that God is good, like the first two servants seem to do?
5. In what ways do you think that God is hard, like the third servant?

6. Do you prioritize faithfulness or success? While the actions externally may not look different, the internal mind-set of faithfulness or success matters to God, and we can ask the Holy Spirit to reorient our perspective.

7. In what ways do you compare yourself with others? How can you invite the Holy Spirit to help you value the way God has made you and the gifts he has given you?

GROWING IN GRACE

*That same day Jesus went out of the house and sat by
the lake. Such large crowds gathered around him that
he got into a boat and sat in it, while all the people stood
on the shore. Then he told them many things in parables, saying: "A farmer went out to sow his seed. As he
was scattering the seed, some fell along the path, and
the birds came and ate it up. Some fell on rocky places,
where it did not have much soil. It sprang up quickly,
because the soil was shallow. But when the sun came
up, the plants were scorched, and they withered because
they had no root. Other seed fell among thorns, which
grew up and choked the plants. Still other seed fell on
good soil, where it produced a crop—a hundred, sixty
or thirty times what was sown. Whoever has ears, let
them hear."*

*The disciples came to him and asked, "Why do you
speak to the people in parables?"*

*He replied, "Because the knowledge of the secrets
of the kingdom of heaven has been given to you, but*

not to them. Whoever has will be given more, and they will have an abundance. Whoever does not have, even what they have will be taken from them. This is why I speak to them in parables:
    "Though seeing, they do not see;
        though hearing, they do not hear or understand.
      In them is fulfilled the prophecy of Isaiah:
    "'You will be ever hearing but never understanding;
        you will be ever seeing but never perceiving.
    For this people's heart has become calloused;
      they hardly hear with their ears,
      and they have closed their eyes.
    Otherwise they might see with their eyes,
      hear with their ears,
      understand with their hearts
    and turn, and I would heal them.'

But blessed are your eyes because they see, and your ears because they hear. For truly I tell you, many prophets and righteous people longed to see what you see but did not see it, and to hear what you hear but did not hear it.

"Listen then to what the parable of the sower means: When anyone hears the message about the kingdom and does not understand it, the evil one comes and snatches away what was sown in their heart. This is the seed sown along the path. The seed falling on rocky ground refers to someone who hears the word and at once receives it with joy. But since they have no root, they last only a short time. When trouble or persecution comes because of the word, they quickly fall away. The seed falling among the thorns refers to someone

who hears the word, but the worries of this life and
the deceitfulness of wealth choke the word, making it
unfruitful. But the seed falling on good soil refers to
someone who hears the word and understands it. This
is the one who produces a crop, yielding a hundred,
sixty or thirty times what was sown."

INTRODUCTION

What do you do when something does not live up to your expectations? When something is different from what you expected? When this happens we are often disappointed, even resentful, that we do not get what we want. However, when we cannot change something—or someone—to become what we expect, we have another choice. We can accept the way things are.

My younger stepdaughter recently got married. She knew early on when she met James that she wanted to marry him. After dating for about a year, they took a trip to England, where his family lives. She was certain he would propose to her there, but day after day went by, and there was no proposal. In her mind, their trip to England had been the perfect setting, and surely if he were going to do it, it would have been then. Disappointed, she concluded that maybe he wasn't going to propose at all.

What she did not know was that all this time James had been planning to propose a couple of months later. His parents would be in Southern California to visit his sister, and so Jordan and James would take the opportunity to visit as well. Since this was where we lived, this meant that a good portion of both families would be on hand. He made arrangements to propose to her on a local beach, followed by a surprise brunch at a place overlooking the ocean where all of us would be waiting to celebrate with them. The plan went off beautifully, and Jordan later agreed that it was even better than she had expected.

We all live with expectations. Sometimes they are met, but more often things are much different than we had planned or hoped for. How do you react when things don't happen as you would like? Do you let your frustration get the best of you? Does your disappointment hinder your ability to enjoy what is actually there? Do you recognize opportunities that come in unexpected packages, or do you pass them by because you are busy looking for something else?

We see the problem of living with inflexible expectations in the Gospels. The kingdom that Jesus proclaims is not like what the Jews expect. This meas that people have a choice. They can reject Jesus and his message, or they can see that they were mistaken, accept his message for what it is, and so receive Jesus and the kingdom he proclaims. The parables Jesus tells play an important part in communicating to people what the kingdom is going to be like. What will their response be? What is our response?

THE PARABLE

In the parable of the sower, Jesus uses an image that would have been well known to his audience. The people depended on farmers having a good harvest, and so they would all have an interest in what would provide a bountiful crop.[1]

In Jesus' parable, a farmer sows seed, which lands in different types of soil. Some seed lands on the path and is eaten by birds. Traditionally a field would be plowed to a depth of one to three inches. The farmer would walk up and down the rows, scattering the seed in the furrows before plowing again to cover it. Some would accidentally land on the

---

1. David Wenham, *The Parables of Jesus* (Downers Grove, IL: InterVarsity, 1989), 41–42.

hard paths surrounding the fields, making it easy for birds to come and eat it.[2]

Other seed lands on rocky soil, a common feature in the Galilean hillsides. In these places, there would have been only a thin layer of soil over the rocks, not enough for the seeds to grow.[3] The seeds would sprout under these conditions, but since they could not set deep roots they would be quickly scorched by the hot sun and wither.

Some falls among thorns. The thorns might have been unknown to the farmer when he sowed.[4] However, when the seeds try to grow, they must compete for nutrients from the soil with the thorny plants that are already there.[5] As a result, they are not able to get enough nutrition. They do not necessarily die, but they are not able to produce grain.[6]

Finally, some seed falls on good soil. Having the proper nutrients and able to take firm root, the seed springs forth and yields an abundant harvest—thirtyfold, sixtyfold, even one hundredfold.

Jesus' explanation of the parable is straightforward: the different types of soil refer to the hearts of people who hear the gospel. The path, not the seed, is like the hearts of those who receive the gospel only superficially. It does not take root, and Satan quickly snatches it away. The seed on the rocky soil may seem to take root, but because there is no depth, the person falls away as soon as troubles or persecution arise. Some seed is able to take root firmly, but is choked by the "thorns" of life, such as the cares of the world or desire for wealth, and

---

2. Michael J. Wilkins, *Matthew*, NIV *Application Commentary* (Grand Rapids: Zondervan, 2004), 475.

3. Leon Morris, *The Gospel according to Matthew*, Pillar New Testament Commentaries (Grand Rapids: Eerdmans, 1992), 134.

4. Wenham, *Parables of Jesus*, 42.

5. Wilkins, *Matthew*, 475.

6. R. T. France, *Matthew*, New International Commentary on the New Testament (Grand Rapids: Eerdmans, 2007), 505.

ultimately is unfruitful. It is only the seed that falls on the good soil that is able to yield an abundant harvest for the kingdom.

RESPONDING TO THE PARABLE

Although the story is usually called the parable of the sower, the focus is not so much on the sower, but on the soils. Each person must cultivate the right type of soil for the kingdom to take root and grow abundantly.

You probably recognize the different types of responses to the gospel in your own experience or the experiences of those you know. Some may hear the gospel, but do not understand it or simply reject it outright. Others may receive it enthusiastically, but when persecution or other problems come up, they give up in disappointment, discouragement, or disgust. Still others respond to the gospel, but the word becomes choked and unfruitful in their lives because it competes with the cares and desires of the world. But some, even though it may take time, grow steadily, bear much fruit, and become faithful disciples of the kingdom.

Even when one has accepted the gospel, there are still many dangers that threaten the fruitfulness of the plant. Being a disciple is not simply a one-time commitment, but requires proper care for the seed God plants in our hearts to glow and flourish.

My husband has spent countless hours in our backyard garden breaking up the hard clay and replacing it with good, moist soil. He watches carefully to see how the plants respond to the amount of water he gives, and he plucks the weeds that grow up between the plants. It takes time, but the result is a beautiful array of flowers, a thriving avocado tree, and a peaceful back yard, where we spend hours relaxing with family and friends, reading quietly, and praying as we gaze at the plants and watch the birds drink from the fountain.

We have a responsibility to provide a similarly hospitable environment for the gospel to grow in our lives. But how do we do this, and what precisely is that good soil?

GOING DEEPER INTO THE PARABLE

An important clue for understanding the soil occurs in the way Jesus tells the parable. What we often do not notice is that in between the telling of the parable itself and the explanation, the disciples approach Jesus and ask him why he speaks to the crowd in parables. Jesus answers by telling them that while they have been given "the secrets of the kingdom of heaven," these have not been given to the crowds.[7] Not all will understand, and Jesus explains that some have closed off their hearts to his message.

Then, to illustrate his point, Jesus gives the explanation to the disciples. In other words, he tells the parable to the crowds, but only the disciples get to hear what it actually means.

Jesus' teachings were not always easy to understand. We see this throughout the Gospels, such as when Jesus tells the disciples that he must die, and Peter responds that this will never happen to him. Jesus' response of "Get behind me, Satan!" is the surefire clue Peter has definitely misunderstood something (Matt 16:21–23).

Here, though, we see the disciples pursue Jesus in order to get the meaning of the parable, which they do not quite grasp. They demonstrate the openness of their hearts when they approach Jesus with their question. Their reward is to receive the explanation of the parable.[8]

---

7. The Greek word for "secrets" is *mystērion*, which can also be translated as "mystery." In Scripture the term generally refers to what can only be known by divine revelation, as opposed to natural human insight. Since the English word "mystery" more often refers to something that is obscure or puzzling, "secret" is probably a better way to understand the term (France, *Gospel of Matthew*, 511).

8. We see this again when Matthew relates that Jesus' use of parables is to fulfill "what was spoken through the prophet, 'I will open my mouth in parables, I will

In order to really understand the gospel, we must be open to God's teaching, which may not be what we expect or can comprehend on our own. Paul comes straight out and says it is impossible for humans on their own to understand God's ways: "We declare God's wisdom, a mystery that has been hidden and that God destined for our glory before time began ... as it is written: 'What no eye has seen, what no ear has heard, and what no mind has conceived'—the things God has prepared for those who love him—these are the things God has revealed to us by his Spirit" (1 Cor 2:7–10).

In order to hear properly, we must remember that God's secrets must be given to us. This means a primary task is to be ready to receive the revealed message. This is why the soils matter. The message will be received differently according to the type of "soil" found in each person's heart. The hearer must have the humility to receive what God gives, even if it is different from what one expects.

We see how the parable finds fertile soil in the disciples' hearts, as seen in their willingness to pursue Jesus. Though they might be confused about the nature of the kingdom he proposes, they are willing to listen and ask Jesus about the parables. However, throughout the Gospels we see how people are unwilling to accept the true kingdom Jesus is proposing. In one example, John 6:15 says that the people want to make him king by force, which would have made him a ruler on the same level as Herod or the Romans.[9] Through the influence of the

---

utter things hidden since the creation of the world'" (Matt 13:34–35, in reference to the parable of the wheat and the weeds in Matt 13:24–30). The reference comes from Ps 78:2. France notes that the author, traditionally known as Asaph, while not a prophet himself, "is understood to be making a prophetic utterance" (*Gospel of Matthew*, 530). Asaph's prophetic statement is an account of Israel's history with the purpose to teach them not to repeat the mistakes of their forefathers, "a stubborn and rebellious generation, whose hearts were not loyal to God, whose spirits were not faithful to him" (Ps 78:8). Again, the disciples approach Jesus, this time explicitly asking for an explanation after the crowds leave, to which Jesus responds by giving them what they ask.

9. Gary M. Burge, *John, NIV Application Commentary* (Grand Rapids: Zondervan, 2000), 194–95.

Pharisees, the crowds that follow Jesus in his early days and respond to the miracles eventually reject the kingdom Jesus proposes. They even become so hardened that they end up calling for his execution and supporting the release of the rebel Barabbas instead. Barabbas had taken part in an uprising against Rome, and his goals were more in line with the establishment of the physical kingdom of Israel the Jews wanted.[10]

What is the nature of the kingdom that Jesus proclaims? A big part is that it was not about earthly power, conquest, and status, but rather the power of grace.

THE IMPORTANCE OF THE SOIL OF THE HEART

Jesus came not only to establish his earthly kingdom, but also to reign in people's hearts. He would not only conquer Satan, but he would also rescue people from the poison of sin. The parable teaches us that the condition of our hearts matters in receiving the gospel message. The gospel can only flourish in good soil.

The passages right before our parable prepare us for understanding what this good soil is like. We read about Jesus' increasing conflicts with the Pharisees. They twice accuse him of violating the Sabbath, but Jesus responds each time by explaining how they misunderstand the intent of the law, which is to serve God's people and not the other way around.[11] In the first instance, Jesus' disciples pick and eat grain on the Sabbath. Jesus replies that even David ate the consecrated bread when he was fleeing from Saul, as told in 1 Samuel 21:1–6. God desires "mercy, not sacrifice" (Matt 12:7).

---

10. Wilkins, *Matthew*, 492. Luke says that Barabbas had been imprisoned for insurrection and murder (23:18; see also Mark 15:7; John 18:40). Craig A. Evans notes that it is difficult to know which rebellion Barabbas took part in. See Evans, *Mark 8:27–16:29, Word Biblical Commentary 34B* (Nashville: Thomas Nelson, 2001), 481.

11. Wilkins, *Matthew*, 440.

In the second incident, Jesus heals the man with the withered hand and says the point is not so much whether it is lawful to heal on the Sabbath, but that it is lawful to do good on the Sabbath (12:9–13). This is the higher principle that should be followed.

What is the Pharisees' response to Jesus' interpretation of the law according to such mercy? They conclude he is a heretic and begin to plot to kill him (12:14).[12]

Matthew's Gospel shows us how everyone must make a decision about Jesus. The Pharisees have the evidence in front of them, and they can decide to follow or reject him. They decide that he is an imposter, even an agent of Satan (12:23–24). The question is, then, What will the crowds think, since they look to the Pharisees as their leaders? At this critical juncture Jesus uses the parables to compel them to make a decision, to follow him as the Messiah or to follow the Pharisees.

This is certainly not an easy decision for the crowds, as the Pharisees are their religious leaders. While it can be easy on our part to shake our heads at the Jews who did not follow Jesus, we also have to recognize how difficult it would be to change powerful and long-held ideas and then, in addition, to go against those whom they have depended on for religious leadership.

Jesus challenges their most fundamental ideas. One well-known example is when Jesus redefines what it means to be part of his "family." The key group in the ancient world was the family, but Jesus directly confronts their deeply held ideas about the family.[13] He speaks to the crowd, who inform him that his mother and brothers are waiting

---

12. The Pharisees would not have taken such extreme action simply over a difference in how to interpret the law. Rather, this stems from Jesus' claim to be the messianic "Son of Man" and "Lord of the Sabbath" (Matt 12:8), who has the authority to give the true interpretation of the law. To them, Jesus is guilty of heresy and should be put to death (Wilkins, *Matthew*, 441–43).

13. Joseph H. Hellerman, *When the Church Was a Family* (Nashville: B&H Academic, 2009), 6.

for him. Jesus responds by saying that those who do the will of God are his true mother and brother and sister (Matt 12:46–50). In other words, it is obedience to God's call in Jesus that matters, not bloodline. This event comes right before the parable of the sower, preparing Jesus' audience by letting them know that the kingdom is radical and accepting it is hard.

Because of the challenges, Jesus shows that it all begins with a heart that is ready to receive whatever God has rather than one that insists on holding on to the way one thinks things ought to be. More than being a Jew, one must have a heart made up of good soil that responds to the gospel itself and not our own ideas of what it should be.[14]

THE IMPORTANCE OF THE HEART

I suspect I am not the only one who easily forgets to think about the condition of my heart. Instead, I get caught up in doing and forgetting that doing flows out of what is in the heart. Jesus makes it clear that "the mouth speaks what the heart is full of" (Matt 12:34). Proverbs warns us of the importance of the heart as well, by telling us to "guard" our heart, "for everything you do flows from it" (Prov 4:23).

When I first became a Christian, for example, I remember thinking that while Jesus had forgiven me of my sins, it was now up to me to make sure I didn't continue to do the things that made me need forgiveness in the first place. I see this type of thinking frequently in my students, too. They often express their concern that they need to "present" themselves to God and feel shame when they are not able to live up to what they see as God's expectations for them.

---

14. This also helps us understand Jesus' comment in Matt 5:20, where he tells the crowd, "unless your righteousness surpasses that of the Pharisees and the teachers of the law, you will certainly not enter the kingdom of heaven." It is not following the external law that matters, but receiving Christ's righteousness and God's work of inner transformation.

But if we needed saving in the first place, doesn't it make sense that it is impossible for us to present ourselves to God as "perfect"? Perhaps what our salvation in Christ teaches us is that what we need is not just forgiveness, but dependence on God and submission to his working in our lives. Perhaps presenting ourselves to God as imperfect, but willing to let him change us, is where we need to be. And so perhaps this is why the heart is so important.

We see an example of this type of heart in David after his sin with Bathsheba (2 Sam 11). If you want to talk about not being perfect, I suspect that most of us will not come close to David's sin with Bathsheba. After he commits adultery with her, he arranges for her husband to be killed. Then, after realizing he has arranged for an innocent man's death, does David feel remorse? It sure doesn't seem like it. He seems to think instead that this is a terrific opportunity to make Bathsheba his wife! David's heart remains hardened until God sends the prophet Nathan to confront him.

However, God is able to cut through David's defenses with—you guessed it—a parable.

The parable goes like this:

> There were two men in a certain town, one rich and the other poor. The rich man had a very large number of sheep and cattle, but the poor man had nothing except one little ewe lamb he had bought. He raised it, and it grew up with him and his children. It shared his food, drank from his cup and even slept in his arms. It was like a daughter to him.
>
> Now a traveler came to the rich man, but the rich man refrained from taking one of his own sheep or cattle to prepare a meal for the traveler who had come to him. Instead, he took the ewe

lamb that belonged to the poor man and prepared it for the one who had come to him.

(2 Sam 12:1–4)

After Nathan presents the parable, David responds passionately and angrily. He demands severe punishment for the man. "The man who did this must die! He must pay for that lamb four times over, because he did such a thing and had no pity" (2 Sam 12:5–6).

David's overreaction seems to prove the old saying that the thing that bothers you the most in other people is probably what you dislike the most in yourself. His response seems a bit disproportionate to the offense, which is bad, but hardly deserving of the death penalty. But Nathan brings everything back on David by announcing, "You are that man!" The condemnation David pronounced on the person in the story now comes back to condemn him. At that moment, David knows he has nowhere to hide. He has come face to face with his sin.

But here is the point. What David learns from this profoundly shattering and humbling experience is that he is a person of great pride and arrogance, capable of committing the most atrocious sins. He also learns that the way through his sinfulness is to depend utterly on the mercy of God and allow God to work through him. What David learns is that God desired not perfection, but a "broken spirit, a broken and contrite heart" (Ps 51:16–17). When confronted, he gives in, and when he gives in, he is able to receive from God and be changed.

It was a far different case with the Pharisees. They were experts in the law and renowned for their strict adherence to the law. But Jesus pronounces a different way into the kingdom of God. In Matthew 5:20 he declares that one's righteousness must exceed that of the Pharisees, a statement that would have been shocking to people who knew the Pharisees' diligence in keeping the law. The point is Jesus proclaimed that righteousness comes from grace, not from effort. As a result, righteousness works from the "inside-out" rather than "outside-in."[15]

In fact, Jesus condemns the Pharisees for appearing righteous on the outside without allowing God to cleanse them from the inside: "Woe to you, teachers of the law and Pharisees, you hypocrites! You are like whitewashed tombs, which look beautiful on the outside but on the inside are full of the bones of the dead and everything unclean. In the same way, on the outside you appear to people as righteous but on the inside you are full of hypocrisy and wickedness" (Matt 23:27–28).

In the kingdom, people will follow the law not simply as an external regulation, which would be impossible to keep, but instead as an internal law. As Jeremiah proclaims, "I will put my law in their minds and write it on their hearts" (31:33). Through the Spirit, God's people will experience a change in their hearts and minds. They will be given a "new heart" and a "new spirit," which will enable them to obey God (Ezek 36:26–27).[16] The result is that "they will all know me, from the least of them to the greatest" (Jer 31:34).

In his arguments with the Pharisees, Jesus says it is the heart, not religious purity, that matters. He says, "Nothing outside a person can defile them by going into them. Rather, it is what comes out of a person that defiles them. ... For it is from within, out of a person's heart, that evil thoughts come—sexual immorality, theft, murder, adultery, greed, malice, deceit, lewdness, envy, slander, arrogance and folly. All these evils come from inside and defile a person" (Mark 7:15–23). This would have challenged the Pharisees, who seem to assume that if the

---

15. Wilkins, *Matthew*, 231.

16. All of this, of course, is based on our forgiveness in Christ. As Charles L. Feinberg summarizes, "Basic to obedience is inner knowledge of God's will coupled with an enablement to perform it, all founded on the assurance that sins are forgiven." "Jeremiah," *The Expositor's Bible Commentary*, gen. ed. Frank E. Gaebelein (Grand Rapids: Zondervan, 1986), 6:576.

outside is clean, the inside will be clean as well. But for Jesus, the point is an internal righteousness that begins with the heart.[17]

Although we may look down on the Pharisees for their rigid adherence to the law, which prevents them from seeing the beauty of the gospel Jesus preaches, we can certainly also fall into our own legalistic understandings. How often do we think having a proper spirituality lies in having the correct positions on the various issues of the day, such as abortion or sexuality? How often do we gauge "how we are doing" based on which movies we watch or the music we listen to? How easy it is for us to think that we are "growing" because we do the "right" things without allowing the gospel to deeply penetrate our hearts! Focusing on external actions is a trap we can all fall too easily into.

But we can ask God to help us be attentive to the condition of our hearts.

CONCLUSION: GRACE AND THE GOOD HEART

If we want to know who we really are, we need to look at our hearts. Proverbs 27:19 tells us, "As water reflects the face, so one's life reflects the heart." The heart is who we truly are.[18]

If you picture an iceberg, you see only the top sticking up out of the water. Most of it—over 90 percent—remains underneath. In the same way, most of what is in our hearts lies beneath the surface and yet determines the course of our lives. As Proverbs 4:23 warns us, "Above all else, guard your heart, for everything you do flows from it." We would be wise to consider what Luke 6:45 tells us of how our lives reflect our hearts: "A good man brings good things out of the good

---

17. Wilkins, *Matthew*, 232.

18. Robert L. Saucy, *Minding the Heart* (Grand Rapids: Kregel, 2013), 31. He also refers to the heart as the "deep core of the person" and says that in Scripture, "'heart' is often a synonym for 'self'" (36–37).

stored up in his heart, and an evil man brings evil things out of the evil stored up in his heart. For the mouth speaks what the heart is full of."[19]

So we see how important it is to take care of our hearts. When the world shouts competing beliefs about who we are and what we should believe, it becomes more important than ever to find our guidance in what God says. We can be like the psalmist, who declares that he has "hidden your word in my heart that I might not sin against you" (Ps 119:11). We can follow the admonition of the writer of Proverbs, who urges us to keep God's word "within your heart" (Prov 4:21) and "always on your heart" (Prov 6:21).

When the word finds fertile ground in our hearts, our hearts in turn become even more receptive to God's transforming truth. As one scholar describes, "the more of God's revealed truth that we assimilate, the more our capacity for assimilating truth will grow, in a sort of spiritual geometric progression." Similarly, the more we harden our hearts, the easier it is to harden them further, as the "capacity for apprehension and appropriation of spiritual truth dwindles until it disappears."[20]

In other words, we are continually given the opportunity to harden or soften our hearts, and each decision contributes to the future condition of our hearts. Knowing and accepting how God works by grace is a critical part of what keeps our hearts soft toward God.

If we look at the example of the disciples, we see that the disciples did not necessarily do everything perfectly or understand completely. Paul struggles with his "thorn" in his flesh and eventually learns that rather than removing the thorn, what God does is give him grace. In Paul's weakness, God provides strength.

---

19. Ecclesiastes 10:2 explains, "The heart of the wise inclines to the right, but the heart of the fool to the left."

20. Alan Cole, *The Gospel according to St. Mark: An Introduction and Commentary*, Tyndale New Testament Commentary (Grand Rapids: Eerdmans, 1961), 148.

The soil is only what receives the seed. It is neither the seed nor what causes growth. In other words, we cannot cause our own spiritual growth. As Paul says in 1 Corinthians in regard to the "seed" that he planted, only God "makes things grow" (3:6–7). As we continue to ponder the lessons of the parables, we are also challenged to allow God to use the parables to pierce our defenses and open us to God's works of grace in our hearts. Only a broken and contrite heart (Ps 15:17) and Christ in me, the "hope of glory" (Col 1:27), can make me into the person God intended me to be.

MAJOR TAKEAWAYS

1. The four types of soil represent four kinds of people and the way they respond to the message (the seed) of the kingdom.
2. The seed on the path represents the one who does not understand the message, which is then snatched away by Satan.
3. The seed in rocky soil represents the one who initially receives the word, but it is not rooted and so falls away when difficulties arise.
4. The seed in the thorns represents the person who allows the worries of the world and the deceitfulness of riches to choke the word and become unfruitful.
5. The seed in good soil represents the one who produces an abundant kingdom harvest.
6. Jesus tells the disciples that the parables reveal the "mysteries of heaven," and unless the Spirit reveals, we cannot understand them.

7. Only God can make our hearts become good soil as we focus on yielding to him and receiving his grace.
8. Instead of focusing on external rules, as the Pharisees did, we can focus on nurturing our hearts and aligning them with the truth of Scripture.

QUESTIONS

1. In what ways is your heart like the rocky soil? In other words, what are the areas of faith that are not securely rooted in your heart? Why?
2. Consider the seed that grows among the thorns. What worries of the world and other cares and desires are choking your fruitfulness? Why?
3. In what ways is your heart good soil? In other words, in what ways are you yielding to him and his work in your life?
4. Galatians 5:22–23 describes the fruit of the Spirit as "love, joy, peace, forbearance, kindness, goodness, faithfulness, gentleness and self-control." Is your faith bearing fruit? Invite the Spirit to see which areas of your life are particularly fruitful, which ones are not, and why.
5. Are there ways in which a focus on following the law is hindering your faith?
6. What were the Jews' misperceptions about the kingdom, and how did these affect them and their ability to receive Jesus and his message of the kingdom? Ask the Holy Spirit to bring to mind some of your misperceptions and how these affect you.

7. Why is the heart important to a life of faith? How is your heart affecting you? Ask the Lord to show you any false beliefs you are harboring.

EPILOGUE

When we think about the parables as stories that should be responded to rather than simply listened to or learned from, we also realize that Jesus didn't just give commands. He came to change hearts and minds. The challenge of the parables is to allow them to penetrate our defenses, to allow God to expose our hearts, and then to respond to the gentle leading of his Spirit. The parables teach us about the grace of God. But we cannot receive or be changed by his grace unless we are open, and the parables open us up to the work of God and the kingdom.

As Hebrews 4:12 tells us, "The word of God is alive and active. Sharper than any double-edged sword, it penetrates even to dividing soul and spirit, joints and marrow; it judges the thoughts and attitudes of the heart." This is certainly true with the parables.

In a world that prizes results, appearances, and performance, the parables remind us that God cares about each person, that he is patient, and that his grace is boundless. The parables do not teach us as much about what God wants as much as they teach us about God, and they teach us that he is eternally for us.

BIBLIOGRAPHY

Adams, Dwayne H. *The Sinner in Luke*. Evangelical Theological Society Monograph Series. Eugene, OR: Pickwick, 2008.

"Autopsies: Each Church Shooting Victim Was Hit at Least 5 Times." *Chicago Tribune*, December 14, 2016. http://www.chicagotribune.com/news/nationworld/ct-charleston-church-shooting-autopsies-20161214-story.html.

Bailey, Kenneth E. *Jesus through Middle Eastern Eyes: Cultural Studies in the Gospels*. Downers Grove, IL: IVP Academic, 2008.

———. *Poet & Peasant and Through Peasant Eyes*. Combined ed. Grand Rapids: Eerdmans, 1983.

Baker, Howard. *Soul Keeping*. Colorado Springs: NavPress, 1998.

Barnett, Paul. *The Second Epistle to the Corinthians*. New International Commentary on the New Testament. Grand Rapids: Eerdmans, 1997.

Berman, Mark. "'I Forgive You': Relatives of Charleston Church Shooting Victims Address Dylann Roof." *Washington Post*, July 19, 2015. https://www.washingtonpost.com/news/post-nation/wp/2015/06/19/i-forgive-you-relatives-of-charleston-church-victims-address-dylann-roof/?utm_term=.52540db7d58e.

Blomberg, Craig L. *Interpreting the Parables*. Downers Grove, IL: InterVarsity, 1990.

———. *Preaching the Parables: From Responsible Interpretation to Powerful Proclamation*. Grand Rapids: Baker, 2004.

Bock, Darrell L. *Luke 1:1–9:50*. Baker Exegetical Commentary on the New Testament. Grand Rapids: Baker, 1994.

———. *Luke 9:51–24:53.* Baker Exegetical Commentary on the New Testament. Grand Rapids: Baker, 1996.

Burge, Gary M. *John.* NIV Application Commentary. Grand Rapids: Zondervan, 2000.

Carson, D. A. "Matthew." Pages 1–599 in vol. 8 of *The Expositor's Bible Commentary,* gen. ed. Frank E. Gaebelein. Grand Rapids: Zondervan, 1984.

Cole, Alan. *The Gospel according to St. Mark: An Introduction and Commentary.* Tyndale New Testament Commentaries. Grand Rapids: Eerdmans, 1961.

Danker, Frederick W. *Jesus and the New Age.* Philadelphia: Fortress, 1988.

"Dylann Roof's Confession, Journal Details Racist Motivation for Killings." *Chicago Tribune,* December 10, 2016. http://www.chicagotribune.com/news/nationworld/ct-dylann-roof-charleston-shooting-20161209-story.html.

Evans, Craig A. *Mark 8:27–16:29.* Word Biblical Commentary 34B. Nashville: Thomas Nelson, 2001.

Fee, Gordon D., and Douglas Stuart. *How to Read the Bible for All Its Worth.* 4th ed. Grand Rapids: Zondervan, 2014.

Feinberg, Charles L. "Jeremiah." Pages 355–691 in vol. 6 of *The Expositor's Bible Commentary,* gen. ed. Frank E. Gaebelein. Grand Rapids: Zondervan, 1986.

Ferguson, Everett. *Backgrounds of Early Christianity.* 2nd ed. Grand Rapids: Eerdmans, 1993.

France, R. T. *Matthew.* New International Commentary on the New Testament. Grand Rapids: Eerdmans, 2007.

Freedman, David Noel, ed. *Eerdmans Dictionary of the Bible.* Grand Rapids: Eerdmans, 2000.

Bibliography

Green, Joel B. *The Gospel of Luke.* New International Commentary on the New Testament. Grand Rapids: Eerdmans, 1997.

Gurtner, Daniel M. "Noncanonical Jewish Writings." Pages 290–309 in *The World of the New Testament,* edited by Joel B. Green and Lee Martin MacDonald. Grand Rapids: Baker, 2013.

Hagner, Donald A. *Matthew 14–28.* Word Biblical Commentary 33B. Dallas: Word, 1995.

Heflick, Nathan A. "Wanting Less, So Long as Others Don't Get More." *Psychology Today,* March 31, 2017. https:/www.psychologytoday.com/us/blog/the-big-questions/201703/wanting-less-so-long-others-dont-get-more.

Hellerman, Joseph H. *When the Church Was a Family.* Nashville: B&H Academic, 2009.

Hultgren, Arland J. *The Parables of Jesus.* Grand Rapids: Eerdmans, 2000.

Kistemaker, Simon J. *The Parables: Understanding the Stories Jesus Told.* Grand Rapids: Baker, 1980.

Lee-Barnewall, Michelle. "Pharisees, Sadducees, and Essenes." Pages 218–19 in *The World of the New Testament,* edited by Joel B. Green and Lee Martin McDonald. Grand Rapids: Baker, 2013.

Longman, Tremper, III, ed. *The Baker Illustrated Bible Dictionary.* Grand Rapids: Baker, 2013.

Manning, Brennan. *The Ragamuffin Gospel.* Sisters, OR: Multnomah, 1990.

Marshall, I. Howard. *The Gospel of Luke.* New International Greek Testament Commentary. Grand Rapids: Eerdmans, 1978.

Mason, Steve. "Pharisees." Pages 1043–45 in *Eerdmans Dictionary of the Bible*, edited by David Noel Freedman. Grand Rapids: Eerdmans, 2000.

Maxham, Julie C. "Witness, Discipleship, and Hospitality: A Lukan Theology of Women in the Ministry of Jesus." ThM thesis, Talbot School of Theology, 2017.

Morris, Leon. *The Gospel according to Matthew*. Pillar New Testament Commentaries. Grand Rapids: Eerdmans, 1992.

———. *Luke*. Tyndale New Testament Commentaries. Leicester, UK: Inter-Varsity Press; Grand Rapids: Eerdmans, 1988.

Nolland, John. *Luke 9:21–18:34*. Word Biblical Commentary 35B. Dallas: Word, 1993.

Pentecost, J. Dwight. *The Parables of Jesus*. Grand Rapids: Zondervan, 1982.

Platt, Suzy, ed. *Respectfully Quoted: A Dictionary of Quotations*. Washington, DC: Library of Congress, 1989.

Ridderbos, Herman. *Matthew*. Grand Rapids: Zondervan, 1987.

Saucy, Robert L. *Minding the Heart*. Grand Rapids: Kregel, 2013.

Scott, Bernard Brandon. *Hear Then the Parable*. Minneapolis: Fortress, 1989.

Selzer, Richard. *Mortal Lessons: Notes on the Art of Surgery*. New York: Simon & Schuster, 1976.

Snaith, John G. *Ecclesiasticus*. Cambridge: Cambridge University Press, 1974.

Snodgrass, Klyne R. *Stories with Intent: A Comprehensive Guide to the Parables of Jesus*. Grand Rapids: Eerdmans, 2008.

Ten Boom, Corrie, with John and Elizabeth Sherrill. *The Hiding*

Place. Washington Depot, CT: Chosen Books, 1971.

Tippetts, Kara. *The Hardest Peace: Expecting God's Grace in the Midst of Life's Hard.* Colorado Springs: David C. Cook, 2014.

Twelftree, G. H. "Scribes." Pages 732–35 in *Dictionary of Jesus and the Gospels,* edited by Joel B. Green and Scot McKnight. Downers Grove, IL: InterVarsity, 1993.

VanderKam, James C. *An Introduction to Early Judaism.* Grand Rapids: Eerdmans, 2001.

Wenham, David. *The Parables of Jesus.* Downers Grove, IL: InterVarsity, 1989.

Wilkins, Michael J. *Matthew.* NIV Application Commentary. Grand Rapids: Zondervan, 2004.

Wright, Stephen. *Tales Jesus Told: An Introduction to the Narrative Parables of Jesus.* Carlisle, UK: Paternoster, 2002.

Yancey, Philip. *What's So Amazing about Grace?* Grand Rapids: Zondervan, 1997.

Young, Brad H. *The Parables: Jewish Tradition and Christian Interpretation.* Grand Rapids: Baker, 1998.

Youngblood, Ronald F. "1, 2 Samuel." In *Expositor's Bible Commentary,* edited by Frank E. Gaebelein. Grand Rapids: Zondervan, 1992.

SUBJECT/
AUTHOR INDEX

SCRIPTURE INDEX

Old Testament

New Testament

Scripture Index

Apocrypha